Christmas Customs Around the World

BOOKS BY HERBERT H. WERNECKE
Published by The Westminster Press

Christmas Customs Around the World
Christmas Songs and Their Stories
The Book of Revelation Speaks to Us

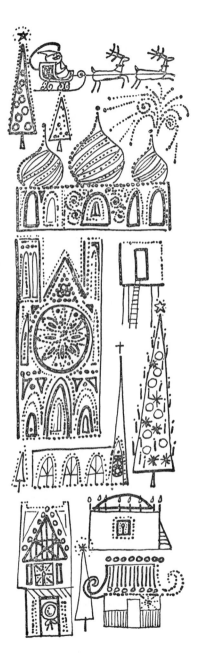

Christmas
Customs
Around
the World

by
Herbert H. Wernecke

THE
WESTMINSTER
PRESS
Philadelphia

Contents

Preface   7

Acknowledgments   9

1. The Origin, Legends, and Customs of Christmas   11

2. Christmas in Europe   43

3. Christmas in the United States and Canada   69

4. Christmas in Central America and the West Indies   80

5. Christmas in South America   89

6. Christmas in Africa   99

7. Christmas in the Middle East   111

8. Christmas in the Far East and the Antipodes   133

9. Recipes from Around the World   153

10. Christmas Customs in Christmas Programs   169

Bibliography   175

Indexes   179

Preface

CHRISTMAS brings joy and light to mankind during the darkest month of the year. Though the days are short and the nights long, the children count the days, the weeks, even the months that precede the happy event that brightens the season. And adults join them in their joy. Industry, music, art, literature, and worship center upon it.

Whenever we feel deeply concerned about the future of humanity, it is well to remember that " the Christmas star remains a reality." God not only loved the world two thousand years ago, he loves it still.

In the volume before us, describing the Christmas customs of sixty-six countries, we join the world-wide fellowship that Christmas has produced and so realize in our experience something of the One World that is implied in the angels' song:

> Glory to God in the highest,
> And on earth peace,
> Good will toward men.

We do well to place ourselves anew, each recurring Christmas season, under its hallowing influence:

WHAT CHRISTMAS DOES TO ME

Bring the candles, light the tree,
There's something Christmas does to me,
It weaves a charm, it casts a spell,
It sheds a warmth I cannot tell.

It melts the years with magic art,
It makes me young again in heart;
I long to give where pity pleads,
I think of friends and human needs,
And thrill with joy as from afar
I hear a song and see a star.
Thank God! — Whatever else may be —
For all that Christmas does to me.

— Alfred Grant Walton

Acknowledgments

THOUGH this volume seeks to supplement rather than to duplicate the available information on Christmas customs, many of the facts presented and considerable of the material can lay no claim to originality but is the result of years of filing of newspaper clippings and the like. If any sources have not been duly acknowledged in the body of the book, the author would appreciate having the omission brought to his attention so that proper recognition may be given in future editions.

Special thanks are extended to Mrs. Marian O'Brien, Food Editor of the *St. Louis Globe Democrat*, who offered numerous suggestions for Chapter 9.

We are grateful also to the Editors of the Lutheran *Missionary Outlook* and *Presbyterian Survey* for permission to quote from their periodicals; and to Mrs. Conway T. Wharton, Editorial Assistant of the Board of World Missions of the Presbyterian Church in the U.S., for permission to quote from letters of missionaries of her denomination.

The poem " Good Will to Men," by Dorothy Brown Thompson, is used by permission of The Methodist Publishing House; the poem " At Christmas," by Edgar Guest, is from *Collected Verse*, copyright 1947 and reprinted with permission of the author.

1. The Origin, Legends, and Customs of Christmas

IF ALL our festival days had to be given up except one, it is quite probable that the voices of children would mingle with those of adults and sound forth in a mighty chorus in favor of retaining Christmas. Many might be chiefly interested in it as a home-coming family reunion day, others would be interested in the feasting and revelry; but the great majority of people would probably choose this festival day because, in the words of Phillips Brooks:

> The earth has grown old with its burden of care,
>   But at Christmas it always is young,
> The heart of the jewel burns lustrous and fair,
> And its soul full of music breaks forth on the air,
>   When the song of the angels is sung.
>
> It is coming, old earth, it is coming tonight,
>   On the snowflakes which cover thy sod,
> The feet of the Christ-child fall gently and white,
> And the voice of the Christ-child tells out with delight
>   That mankind are the children of God.

On the sad and the lonely, the wretched and poor,
    That voice of the Christ-child shall fall;
And to every blind wanderer opens the door
Of a hope which he dared not to dream of before,
    With a sunshine of welcome for all.

The feet of the humblest may walk in the field
    Where the feet of the holiest have trod,
This, this is the marvel of mortals revealed,
When the silvery trumpets of Christmas have pealed,
    That mankind are the children of God.

Much has been said and written about the commercialization of Christmas. It is necessary to guard constantly against that, but who would really want to miss the weeks of preparation as well as the climaxing religious services, the joyous get-togethers, and the general spirit of " good will among men " when Christmas carols crowd the ether waves of radio and television? In spite of the occasional abuse of the season, everyone may find a place in his heart and home for the Christ-child. Even the grim specter of war has given way repeatedly to Christmas songs sent across no-man's land to the enemy.

Edgar A. Guest states beautifully for us this universal influence as follows:

A man is at his finest towards the finish of the year;
He is almost what he should be when the Christmas season's here;
Then he's thinking more of others than he's thought the months
    before,
And the laughter of his children is a joy worth toiling for.
He is less a selfish creature than at any other time;
When the Christmas spirit rules him he comes close to the sublime.

Man is ever in a struggle and he's oft misunderstood;
There are days the worst that's in him is the master of the good,
But at Christmas, kindness rules him and he puts himself aside
And his petty hates are vanquished and his heart is opened wide.
Oh, I don't know how to say it, but somehow it seems to me
That at Christmas man is almost what God sent him here to be.

THE ORIGIN AND DEVELOPMENT
OF TODAY'S CHRISTMAS

It is quite generally known that Christmas began as *Christes Masse*, a beloved religious festival originating with the angels' song on Bethlehem's plains, " Glory to God in the highest, and on earth peace, good will toward men." It is less well known that only as late as 350 a specific date was set for the observance of the birthday of Christ, namely, December 25, by Julius I, Bishop of Rome, though tradition says that it has been celebrated since 98, and was ordered to be observed as a solemn feast by Telesphorus, Bishop of Rome, in 137.

Because this season coincided with pagan festivals, attempts to combine pagan and Christian events led to difficulties. The Romans, for example, observed the lavish Saturnalia from the middle of December to the end, honoring their god of agriculture by indulging in much eating, drinking, and visiting, even to the point of masked reveling and riotous celebration on the streets. The Persians observed the winter solstice by a feast revering the sun, kindling the great fires to Mithra, their deity of light. In northern Europe the pagan Teutonic tribes honored Woden by consuming quantities of food and drink during their yuletide season, the time of the rebirth of the sun.

So it is not surprising that Origen (ca. 200) declared that Christ's birthday was not to be put on a par with pagan carnivals, that it was sinful to keep it as " though he were a King Pharaoh." The intermingling of pagan with Christian elements was denounced by Gregory of Nazianzus, who died in 389, by the request to celebrate Christmas " after a heavenly and not an earthly manner," warning against excessive indulgence of feasting, dancing, and dressing in grotesque costumes of animal skins.

When the church found it impossible through repeated bans to abolish all the pagan customs, it " Christianized " a number of them, divested them of their worst features, and finally incorporated them into the Christian observance of Christmas.

This explains quite largely the use of greenery and candles

and other lights for decorating homes. It is the background of the bringing in and burning of the yule log, singing of carols, exchanging of presents, and feasting happily together amid general rejoicing. Although at first Christians were expected to observe the day of Nativity as a religious holiday exclusively, gradually secular, even pagan, elements were added. Therefore, our modern Christmas draws on all mankind for certain elements of its observance, but at the same time it is in danger of becoming, and often has become, a strange medley of Christian and pagan rites.

In England, Christmas is said to have been observed first as a holiday in 521 when King Arthur celebrated his victory in retaking York. The guests at his famous Round Table were entertained by wandering minstrels who glorified the national heroes.

Alfred the Great annually set aside twelve days of yule festivities in the ninth century. In the Norman period, after 1066, Christmas became gayer than ever, entertaining and reveling continuing until Twelfth-night. This continued through the Middle Ages, with sumptuous pageants and masks added.

When the Puritans came into power under Oliver Cromwell, the prevailing Christmas observance was attacked as a heathen practice and Parliament passed an act forbidding the celebration of Christ's Nativity and other religious festivals including Easter and Whitsuntide. Naturally, such an edict was impossible to enforce completely, but this Puritanic spirit can still be detected in religious groups today, both in Europe and in America.

With the restoration of the monarchy under Charles II (1660), the old yuletide customs gradually reappeared but never became as extravagant again. In the Victorian period Charles Dickens' A Christmas Carol both reflected the customs of the time and did much to establish them more firmly and wholesomely.

With the settlement of America by both Puritan and Cavalier types, two distinct emphases prevailed here for a time. To the Jamestown, Virginia, colony, 1607, the pleasure-loving Cavaliers brought from "Merrie England" such holiday customs as the ringing of bells, burning a yule log, dining elaborately, dancing, playing games, and singing carols. Evergreens decorated their homes and churches, and candles were used freely.

A similar spirit pervaded the jolly Dutch settlement in New Amsterdam, later New York. They loved yuletide feasting and merriment, and to their St. Niclaes, San Claas, or Sant Nikolass, we owe our modern Santa Claus.

In contrast we find that the Pilgrims did not have such gay festivities, and that William Bradford reported in his diary in 1620 that on "ye 25th day begane to erect ye first house for comone use to receive them and their goods." The next year Governor Bradford again forbade the observance of the day and commanded that work be continued as on any other day. Apparently his journal reflects correctly the atmosphere that prevailed for some time:

On ye day called Christmas-day, ye Gov'r caled them out to worke (as was used) but ye most of this new company excused themselves, and said it went against their consciences to work on ye day. So ye Gov'r tould them that if they made it a mater of conscience, he would spare them till they were better informed. So he led away ye rest, and left them: but when they came home at noone from their works, he found them in ye streete at play, openly; some pitching ye barr, and some at stoole ball, and such like sports. So he went to them and tooke away their implements, and told them it was against his conscience that they should play, and others worke. If they made ye keeping of it matter of devotion, let them kepe their houses, but there should be no gameing or revelling in ye streets. Since which time nothing hath been attempted that way, at least, openly.

Although the Pilgrims had a less somber outlook, as indicated by their festive celebrations with friendly neighbors, enmity toward holiday joys is expressed clearly in a law passed in 1659:

Whosoever shall be found observing any such day as Christmas and the like, either by forbearing of labor, feasting, or any other way upon such account as aforesaid, every such person so offending shall pay for each offense five shilling as a fine to the country.

Gradually the influence of the more moderate attitude of those belonging to the Church of England led to the repeal of that law in 1681. Five years later a Christmas service was conducted in the Boston Town Hall, but it was not until 1856 that the holiday was legally recognized, and New England actually did not enter enthusiastically into Christmas observances until the second half of the nineteenth century.

LEGENDS CONNECTED WITH CHRISTMAS

Saint Nicholas Becomes Santa Claus

Since Santa Claus is believed by many to be supplanting the Christ-child as the central person in the observance of Christmas, it will be well to sketch at some length the background from which our modern Santa Claus has emerged.

Although the present-day Santa Claus is taken to be a myth, and in his present form certainly must be so understood, there was a real Saint Nicholas, an early Christian bishop who presided over Myra, a city in Asia Minor. Because of his remarkable childhood and his selection while still a youth as a high church official, he has become known as the Boy Bishop. Because of his love for and relationship to children and because of his generosity, many chapels have been dedicated to his memory. Russia took him as its patron saint, as also did Greece. More churches have been named after him than after any of the apostles — three hundred in Belgium, sixty in Rome, and four hundred in England.

Dutch seamen are supposed to have first carried to Europe the reports of the bishop's generosity, as a result of which children in Holland received special presents on December 6. The traditional appearance of Saint Nicholas in Europe is that of a bearded saint riding on a white horse and carrying a basket of gifts for the good children and a bunch of birch rods for the naughty ones.

While the transformation of the name (originally from the Latin, *Sanctus Nicolaus*; the German, *Sankt Nikolaus*; the Dutch, *Sinter Klaas*) into Santa Claus is readily understandable, it is somewhat more difficult to see how a staid saint of long ago should become the chubby, jolly character who too largely rules the Christmas season.

A few facts will clarify this for us. When the Dutch settled New Amsterdam, now New York, they brought along their tradition of Saint Nicholas, even naming their first church, though Protestant, for him — the St. Nicholas Collegiate Church (recently dissolved to make way for real-estate developments). His image had also been placed on the vessel that brought the Dutch settlers, the *Goede Vrouw*. Quite naturally he was represented with a broad-brimmed hat and a long Dutch pipe, and his long churchly robe was replaced by short breeches. This may be viewed as the first significant step in transforming the pallid saint into a chubby cheer-bringer.

The second step came at the beginning of the nineteenth century, through the merging of the English influence on the forms of Christmas observance in New York with the established parades by the Dutch that featured Saint Nicholas. Writing in 1809, Washington Irving pictured Santa Claus as a jolly, chubby fellow riding through the air in a sleigh drawn by reindeer. On February 22, 1835, a literary society was organized by Washington Irving which met that year on December 6, to honor the famous bishop. Long Dutch pipes were smoked, and other early Dutch customs were observed at such meetings.

From this group, through the influences just mentioned, a short, chubby Hollander seems to have become the personification, as to form and spirit, of Santa Claus, which was indelibly enshrined by Dr. Clement C. Moore in his poem " A Visit from St. Nicholas." On December 22, 1822, Dr. Moore, a professor in the General Theological Seminary in New York, read the poem to his children. A visitor in the home was so pleased with the lines that he copied them and had the poem published the next year in the Troy, New York, *Sentinel*.

It is not difficult to relate " a sleigh full of toys " to the unparalleled generosity of the saint, and " the stockings . . . hung by the chimney with care " to the shoes that the children of Amsterdam and of New Amsterdam set in the chimney corners on the eve of December 6; the " sleigh and eight tiny reindeer " reflect Woden's horse, Sleipnir, upon whose back Saint Nicholas still makes his rounds in Holland. Santa's bells may have been suggested to the author as he drove home in his own sleigh one wintry night. The Christmas tree is, of course, not Dutch, but had come to this country, either directly or indirectly, from Germany.

The final significant step in the transformation of Saint Nicholas into Santa Claus is traceable to the vivid presentation of Clement Moore's general conception by the well-known cartoonist, Thomas Nast, in *Harper's Illustrated Weekly*, in 1863. He gave the white-bearded old gentleman his red, fur-trimmed coat.

While it is unfortunate to have Santa Claus become the center of Christmas, he can symbolize for us such generosity and good will as will cause the month of December to become truly filled with light concerning the unspeakable blessings we enjoy, as well as our obligations to one another and a love that will fulfill them.

The Holly and the Ivy

There are more than one hundred and fifty varieties of holly, and it grows in practically all the countries of the world. It was used for centuries for decorative purposes, especially at winter festivals. Because it bore fruit in the winter, it came to be a symbol of immortality.

In connection with Christmas it has come to represent the crown of thorns worn by Christ, the red of the berries representing the blood. In Denmark it is called Christ-thorn.

A legend relates that on the first Christmas night, when the shepherds went to the manger, a little lamb following them was caught by the holly thorns, and the red berries are the blood drops that froze on the branches.

In many yuletide songs the holly was spoken of as the male

and the ivy as the female. The one that was first brought into the house indicated which sex would rule the house that year! An amusing story embodying this idea is told of an English knight who invited his tenants and their wives to dine with him at Christmas. When the last guest was seated, the knight arose and, with a twinkle in his eye, said to the men, representing the holly, " Before you eat, whoever among you is master of your wife shall now take his stand and carol before the assembly." Finally one timid man arose and sang a short carol.

Then the command was given to the women's table: " Ivy, it is now your turn. Whichever of you is master of her husband, let her sing a carol as proof." Whereupon " they fell all to such a singing that there was never heard such a caterwauling piece of music." The knight then laughed heartily and shouted merrily, " The ivy, the ivy is the master! "

The Mistletoe

The most plausible explanation of the name of the mistletoe is that it is derived from *misteltān,* meaning " different twig," since it grows on trees as a semiparasite and contrasts with them by its huge, dense, light-green growth.

In ancient Britain it was the sacred plant of the Druids, the archdruid and his priests performing elaborate ceremonies around it at the winter solstice. Because of these pagan associations, the mistletoe has seldom been sanctioned for use in church decorations, but it is very commonly found in the homes.

" Give me a kiss " is its meaning in the language of flowers. As it hangs in the doorway or under the chandelier, each lad may claim a kiss from the girl who happens to be under it, removing a berry and giving it to the girl. When all the berries are taken, no more kisses are available.

Probably this custom is a survival of some early marriage rite.

Joseph and the Cherry Tree

A legend that goes back five hundred years or more tells us of Joseph as an old man walking with his young bride in a cherry garden. When she tells him of the visits by the angel, Joseph becomes suspicious and refuses to pick cherries for his wife. Upon Mary's request the branches of the tree bend over graciously for her. Joseph is stricken with remorse and asks forgiveness.

For the complete carol of fourteen verses based on the legend, see Wernecke, *Christmas Songs and Their Stories*, page 27.

Tinsel on the Tree

A beautiful legend seeks to explain why our Christmas trees are decorated with tinsel. Many years ago a good woman with a large family of children prepared the Christmas tree, trimming it profusely. During the night spiders visited the tree and crawled from branch to branch, leaving their beautiful webs behind them. To reward the woman for her goodness, the Christ-child blessed the tree, and all the spider webs were transformed into shining silver.

The Legend of the Christmas Rose

Legend says that a little shepherd girl of Bethlehem followed after the shepherds who had received the angels' message and were journeying to the manger. All the shepherds took along gifts for the Christ; but the little girl had no gift to give. As she lagged behind the others, somewhat sad at heart, there suddenly appeared an angel in a glow of light who scattered beautiful white roses in her path. Eagerly she gathered them in her arms and laid them at the manger as her gift to the little Lord Jesus.

SYMBOLS OF CHRISTMAS COMMONLY USED

" O Tannenbaum, O Tannenbaum! "

It is estimated that in two thirds of the homes in the United States, lighted Christmas trees form the center of holiday observance. In one year, recently, more than twenty-one million trees were sold for about $50,000,000. While President Theodore Roosevelt discouraged their use in the interest of conservation of natural resources, it is now recognized that they can be grown and replaced almost as easily, though not quite so rapidly, as the Christmas turkey.

While it is quite plausible that Luther did provide a fir tree with lighted candles for his family, lighted and decorated trees apparently date back centuries earlier. Primitive tribes revered trees and adorned them in their homes to bring the world of nature indoors. The Egyptians brought the green date palms indoors, for they signified to them life triumphant over death. The Romans trimmed trees with trinkets and toys during the Saturnalia. The Druids honored Odin (or Woden) by tying gilded apples and other offerings on tree branches.

When these peoples accepted Christianity, they continued these winter rites but gradually changed them to honor Christ. So the evergreen tree came to signify Christ bringing new life to the world after the longest dark days of winter. No doubt Luther did much toward making the Christmas tree popular in Germany in the sixteenth century. Even today in Germany the popular carol "O Tannenbaum" ranks second next to "Silent Night! Holy Night!" The full text of both (the version of the former with a more religious note than appears in the original) is to be found in the author's volume *Christmas Songs and Their Stories*, pages 80 and 101 respectively.

The tree soon became popular in Germany, and its use spread to Finland, Denmark, Sweden, and Norway by the nineteenth century. Austria is said to have enjoyed the first tree when Princess Henriette provided one for Vienna in 1816. In 1840, Princess Helene of Mecklenburg brought one to Paris. While a few individuals, generally Germans living in England, had used a few trees in England as early as 1829, the idea really took hold in England only after Prince Albert of Saxe-Coburg, the German-born husband of Queen Victoria, set up a Christmas tree at Windsor Castle in 1841 to carry out the tradition of his native land. Others soon followed, and now the tree is practically as common there as in Germany and in the United States.

Although it is not certain who should be given the honor of having introduced the tree into our country, it seems clear that Charles Follen, a German professor at Harvard, provided a tree for his son each year, beginning in 1832. The first Christmas tree in a church seems to have been provided by a Pastor Henry Schwan, in 1851, in Cleveland, Ohio. During the decades when services were conducted in the German language, the song "The Christmas Tree, the Fairest Tree" was a favorite, since it expresses the positive Christian note based on the Nativity story in Luke. That, too, has been made available in both the original and in its English translation in *Christmas Songs and Their Stories*, page 29.

Not only has the tree been welcomed almost universally into the churches and homes of our country, it is likewise becoming increasingly popular as a center of community observances of the season. Of the nationally famous ones, the following will indicate, with dates, the elaborate preparations for and the appreciative reception of this practice:

1909 — Pasadena, California, decorated a tall tree on Mount Wilson, towering over the city.

1912 — "The Tree of Light," a 60-foot balsam fir, was placed in Madison Square Park in New York.

1913 — "The Children's Christmas Tree," a 75-foot Norway spruce, was placed in Independence Square, Philadelphia.

1920 — "Christmas Tree Lane," a mile-long avenue in Altadena, a suburb of Pasadena, bordered by gigantic, graceful deodar cedars, whose branches spread out forty to fifty feet, planted as seedlings by the sons of Captain Frederick J. Woodbury, is lighted with more than 10,000 multicolored bulbs and enjoyed by millions, including visitors from abroad.

1924 — "The National Living Christmas Tree," planted near the White House, in Sherman Square, Washington, D.C., is lighted each year by the President with suitable ceremonies.

1926 — "The Nation's Christmas Tree," a *Sequoia gigantea*, 267 feet high, more than 3,500 years old, its first limb 130 feet from the ground, a trunk with a circumference of 107 feet, standing in Kings Canyon National Park, in the center of

California, 54 miles from Sanger, provides an appealing setting for annual pilgrimages and Christmas programs.

1933 — Rockefeller Center, New York City, provides trees as high as 90 feet, with unusual ornaments and lighting effects enjoyed by some two and one half million people annually.

1948 — Los Angeles erected a 96-foot white spruce in Pershing Square.

1948 — Bellingham, Washington, celebrated around a 134-foot Douglas fir and the following season used one 153 feet in height.

1950 — Northport, a shopping center near Seattle, holds the record for the tallest tree used, 212 feet high, weighing 25 tons.

Some cities provide somewhat unique forms of trees. Minneapolis fashions one from water pipes, attached like spokes of a wheel to a telephone pole. In 1947, 135 smaller Christmas trees were inserted into the pipes as limbs making a tree 65 feet high. Bethlehem, Pennsylvania, decorates its Hill-to-Hill Bridge with more than 150 spruces and 1,200 electric lights. Its span is dominated by a 60-foot tree composed of many small trees.

If the "immortality" of the evergreen branches and "the Light of the World" is even faintly conveyed, all these elaborate preparations can be genuinely inspiring and exceedingly worth-while.

THE CHRISTMAS TREE

The oak is a strong and stalwart tree,
　　And it lifts its branches up,
And catches the dew right gallantly
　　In many a dainty cup:
And the world is brighter and better made
　　Because of the woodman's stroke,
Descending in sun, or falling in shade,
　　On the sturdy form of the oak.
But stronger, I ween, in apparel green,

And trappings so fair to see,
With its precious freight for small and great,
Is the beautiful Christmas tree.

The elm is a kind and goodly tree,
With its branches bending low:
The heart is glad when its form we see,
And we list to the river's flow.
Ay, the heart is glad and the pulses bound,
And joy illumes the face,
Whenever a goodly elm is found
Because of its beauty and grace.
But kinder, I ween, more goodly in mien,
With branches more drooping and free,
The tint of whose leaves fidelity weaves,
Is the beautiful Christmas tree.

— *Hattie S. Russell*

The Feast of Lights

From early times light has meant faith and intelligence, and it has long been a symbol of Christian joy which dispels the darkness of paganism. Torches, watch fires, beacon lights, and lamps often accompanied joyous occasions and festivities. The Romans, during their Saturnalia, fastened candles to trees, indicating the sun's return to the earth. The Jews have celebrated an eight-day Feast of Lights since pre-Christian times commemorating their victory for religious freedom.

The Christian use of candles symbolizing Christ as the Light of the World seems to be then a combination of Roman and Hebrew customs. As early as 492, Pope Gelasius established Candlemas Day as the time for blessing candles in the churches. Since then it also commemorates the presentation of Jesus in the Temple by his parents, when Simeon greeted him as " a light to lighten the Gentiles " (Luke 2:32).

In medieval Europe the custom arose of lighting a giant Christmas candle that would serve to shed its glow on the festivities until Twelfth-night. Martin Luther is credited with placing tapers on the tree. Since his day, not only has the candle come to be used ever more widely in the homes, on mantels and window sills, but candlelight carol and Communion services have gained favor. One of the most impressive candle services, including organ and orchestral music, the reading of the Christmas story, prayers, and carols, is held each year in the Central Moravian Church, very appropriately at Bethlehem, Pennsylvania. It was started in 1741, when Count Nicholas von Zinzendorf led his people, with a lighted candle in his hand, into a cabin and named their settlement Bethlehem to honor the Christ-child. While electric lights have replaced candles on trees especially, in 1950 America spent $13,000,000 for more than 150,000,000 candles for church and home use.

Mammoth and artistic displays of colored lights are common throughout our land in homes, churches, and public places. The area near Chicago's old water tower is beautified by countless lights from a tall Christmas tree. The Country Club Plaza district of Kansas City uses twenty thousand colored lights and sixty miles of wiring to light it for five weeks. Denver uses more than thirty-three thousand lights to illuminate its Civic Center.

Surely the people have seen a great Light, and we are forcefully reminded of Him who dispels the darkness.

> Sing, ye heavens, tell the story,
> Of his glory,
> Till his praises
> Flood with light earth's darkest places!
> — *Philipp Nicolai*

The Star of Bethlehem

The symbolism of the star is less mixed with non-Christian elements than either the tree or the lights. In both the Old Testament and the New Testament, it refers specifically to Christ. In Num. 24:17, his coming was foretold: " There shall come a Star out of Jacob," and, in Rev. 22:16, he is called the " bright and morning star." Then, too, the star is associated with the story of the Wise Men. " When they saw the star, they rejoiced with ex-

ceeding great joy." (Matt. 2:10.) The carol " We Three Kings
of Orient Are " describes the star as

> . . . star of wonder, star of night,
> Star with royal beauty bright,
> Westward leading, still proceeding,
> Guide us to thy perfect light.

In other songs likewise, sacred and secular, the symbolism of
the star finds expression as indicated by several well-known ti-
tles: " Star in the East," " Star of Bethlehem," " The Star of
Midnight," " How Brightly Beams the Morning Star," " O
Lovely Star That Shone so Bright."

It is not surprising, therefore, that, coming to us directly from
sacred story and symbolism, it has found a large place in
churches, in homes, and in community observances of the Nativity season. In the homes it often crowns the Christmas tree,
decorates a window, and adds attractiveness to cookies, Christmas wrappings, and greeting cards.

In darkened churches a brilliant star suddenly flashed on can
be a vivid reminder of the first Christmas night.

In community Christmas lighting it has likewise formed so
substantial a part that in some cases it becomes the chief attraction. Since 1934, Palmer Lake, Colorado, has featured a star that
is five hundred feet in diameter on the side of Sundance Peak.
This " village's symbol of hope for peace on earth " is visible for
twenty miles and thrills people in automobiles and trains as
they pass by. Van Nuys, California, renames its main street
" Bethlehem Star Lane " each December. Between the illuminated star decorations, religious floats and processions depict the
Christmas story. On South Mountain, at the " Christmas City,"
Bethlehem, Pennsylvania, a star is lighted on December 4 with
a public service in Zinzendorf Square and brings joy to thousands
of visitors until January 2.

" Away in a Manger "

While the Christmas tree became the center of Christmas observances in the churches and homes of northern Europe, the

manger, or crib, continues in favor in southern Europe and beyond. In broad outline it seems true to say that the Christmas crib (in France, *crèche*, or cradle; in Italy, *presepio*, or manger; in Germany, *Krippe*, or manger; in Czechoslovakia, *jeslicky*, or manger; in Spain, *Nacimiento*, the Nativity scene) was popularized by Francis of Assisi by setting up a simple manger scene at the little town of Greccio, Italy, in 1224. The " Little Brother of Mankind," as Francis came to be known, wanted the people to understand the sacred truths of Scripture so that they might have a deeper religious experience. So he arranged for the assembling of the necessary properties, including a manger, straw, a live ox and an ass. Real persons took the parts of Mary, Joseph, and the shepherds, and a life-sized wax figure of the Christ-child was placed in the manger.

Shouts of joy from the peasants greeted the words of Francis and the lullabies of the children. The ceremony was so impressive and well received that it was not only repeated year after year but it spread gradually to Spain, Portugal, France, England, and to distant parts of the world.

For a time the manger scene was more popular in Roman Catholic countries, never becoming so widespread in England, for example, as on the Continent. In more recent years Nativity scenes have become increasingly common in Protestant Germany and in the United States. One significant influence in this direction is the Christmas Putz brought from Moravia and Bohemia by colonists who came because of religious persecution to such places as Bethlehem, Pennsylvania, and Salem, North Carolina, noted settlements of Moravians.

So it is not strange that Bethlehem, Pennsylvania, has a large community Putz displayed daily from December 16 to January 2 in the Christian Education Building of the Central Moravian Church. Today many communities, families, churches of varying faiths, and other groups arrange outdoor Nativity scenes. At the University of Missouri, Columbia, the students build a crib which thousands come to see and enjoy. In Baltimore, Maryland, families arrange " Christmas Gardens " under the trees with the Holy Infant in the center.

From simple, crudely constructed forms to the elaborately carved types by artisans of the Black Forest of Germany and by Alois Lang of Oberammergau, millions view anew the scene first beheld by the shepherds.

" Bells, the Opera of the Steeples " (*Victor Hugo*)

Before Christ's birth, bells had been used to announce both happy and sad events. In medieval times, they became associated more largely with yuletide rejoicing. Church bells frequently pealed out on Christmas Eve, announcing the arrival of the joyous celebration. Tradition credits Saint Nicholas with carrying a hand bell on his visits. It is amusing to read that during the Puritan era a crier with a harsh-sounding hand bell went around to remind citizens that no celebration would be allowed, while after Charles the Second's accession, church bells again honored Christmas each Sunday in Advent (the four Sundays before Christmas) and the air was usually filled with their music on Christmas Eve.

John Keble spoke for many when he said:

> Wake me tonight, my mother dear,
> That I may hear
> The Christmas bells, so soft and clear,
> To high and low, glad tidings tell
> How God, the Father, loved us well.

In our time bells are not merely used as indicated above, but we find them on greeting cards, as real bells, or replicas on outdoor wreaths. Mammoth types add to festive community street decorations, bell-shaped ornaments hang on the tree, and bell-shaped cookies are a part of Christmas baking.

Today some of the world-famous bells, especially in Bethlehem and in London, send their music across the ether waves around the globe on Christmas Eve. These and thousands of others make Longfellow's poem a greater favorite than ever:

> I heard the bells on Christmas Day
> Their old, familiar carols play,
> And wild and sweet
> The words repeat
> Of peace on earth, good will to men!

For the complete poem of four verses, see *Christmas Songs and Their Stories*, page 63.

The Yule Log

In the yule log we have once more an element of the Christmas observance that has its roots more in pagan customs than in the Nativity story. It is quite generally agreed that the yule-log custom came to English-speaking people from their Scandinavian forebears and their pagan ceremonies. "Yule" comes from *rol*, a wheel that indicated the changing of the seasons. For many centuries fire had been the symbol of home and safety. Not only was its warmth satisfying but it served to light the homes after the sun went down. When the Celts and Teutons commemorated the return of the sun — the source of light, heat, and even of life itself — fire naturally played a significant part. For the building of immense bonfires, kindling the yule log became a ceremony of considerable detail and significance. The Druids carefully selected a large log, preferably from a fruit-bearing tree, like the apple, and at other times from a long-lasting one, like the oak. At a solemn gathering they blessed and prayed over it, that it might last forever. Generally a piece of the old log was kept to start the fire the next year.

Out of this general and somewhat uncertain background arose the yule-log ceremony, at home in Scandinavian countries, fairly common in England, less so in France and Germany, but gradually winning favor in the United States.

Colored flames can be produced in your fireplace by painting small pieces of wood with the chemicals indicated below and shellac mixed with sawdust. Holes are bored into the log and filled with the chemical according to the color desired.

Violet flame . . . . potassium nitrate
Red flame . . . . strontium nitrate
Crimson flame . . . . potassium nitrate
Yellow flame . . . . table salt
Emerald flame . . . . copper nitrate
Purple flame . . . . lithium chloride
Apple-green flame . . . . barium nitrate
Vivid green flame . . . . borax
Orange flame . . . . calcium chloride
Blue flame . . . . copper sulfate

Heap on more wood! the wind is chill;
But, let it whistle as it will,
We'll keep our merry Christmas still.
　　　　　　— *Sir Walter Scott*

Three places in the United States and Canada are carrying on the formalities of the yule log somewhat reflecting " Merrie England," while a cheery Christmas fire is provided as elaborately as facilities permit. At the Ahwahnee Hotel, in Yosemite National Park, the log is dragged in ceremoniously. At the Empress Hotel in Victoria, British Columbia, choristers in costumes announce the entrance of the immense log. After it is sprinkled with wine and oil, it is lighted with a piece saved from the brand of the preceding year. In Palmer Lake, Colorado, a public yule-log hunt is planned annually.

No doubt one of the reasons for the growing popularity of the yule log is the comfort and inner satisfaction reflected by John Greenleaf Whittier in " Snow-Bound ":

Shut in from all the world without,
We sat the clean-winged hearth about,
Content to let the north-wind roar
In baffled rage at pane and door,
While the red logs before us beat
The frost-line back with tropic heat;
And ever, when a louder blast
Shook beam and rafter as it passed,
The merrier up its roaring draught
The great throat of the chimney laughed.

But in addition to this, the flame of the yule log came to be symbolic of the light that came from heaven when Christ was born. Therefore in many localities the Christmas festivities lasted as long as the log kept glowing. Among colonial planters in Virginia and Maryland the Negro slaves searched for the largest water-soaked logs so the merry season of leisure might last as many days as possible!

CUSTOMS ASSOCIATED WITH CHRISTMAS

The Advent Candles and Wreaths

A native Christian in New Guinea described Advent thus: " At Advent we should try the key to our heart's door. It may have gathered rust. If so, this is the time to oil it, in order that the heart's door may open more easily when the Lord Jesus wants to enter at Christmas time."

The four Sundays preceding Christmas are observed as Advent Sundays in many churches, with a special emphasis on the advent, or coming, of the Lord. To remind people of this season several interesting and helpful devices have come into being. The Advent House, generally made of cardboard, is so constructed as to make it possible to open a window each day of the Advent weeks and find back of it an appropriate Scripture verse.

A second device consists of mounting candles on a slanting board, about four by twelve inches, raised six inches at one end. Four holes are drilled into it for four candles, to be inserted successively on the four Advent Sundays and a larger one at the top for use at Christmas to represent the birth of the Savior.

Slightly more elaborate and proportionately more beautiful is the Advent wreath, which is hung at a convenient place and receives a red candle each Advent Sunday and a larger one on Christmas Day.

The Boar's Head

The boar's head is given considerable prominence in many English dinners to commemorate the legend that a student of Queen's College, Oxford, being attacked by a wild boar on Christmas Day, choked the animal with a copy of Aristotle and triumphantly brought the boar's head to the dinner table, having cut off the head to retrieve the copy of Aristotle.

This tradition led to the annual custom of serving a boar's head at Queen's College in the Christmas season. For further details and the words and story of " The Boar's Head Carol," see *Christmas Songs and Their Stories*, page 19.

Carols and Caroling

Because there are innumerable collections of carols and books about them, it is necessary to refer only to a few frequently forgotten facts that will make us more appreciative of the treasures of Christmas music we possess.

First of all, we ought to remember that the most original writer of Christmas songs was Luke, the author of the Third Gospel, commonly known as The Gospel According to Luke. The hymns of the Nativity in Luke, chs. 1 and 2, are the basis for the many well-known Christmas songs we enjoy each recurring season. Likewise, several of the beloved oratorios, outstandingly Handel's *The Messiah*, find their inspiration and content in the Christmas message of prophecy and fulfillment as portrayed in the Old and the New Testaments.

Secondly, it is well to take note of the growing interest in community carol-singing and caroling for shut-ins, for strangers away from home, in welfare institutions, in hotels, bus and railroad stations, and for homes where a candle in the window serves as an invitation.

In the city of St. Louis, the Christmas Carolers' Association has, for several decades, organized groups to bring cheer to the lonely and to serenade friends and neighbors, receiving gifts for nondenominational causes. This activity began in 1911 under the auspices of the Children's Aid Society. Through the years the interest has increased to the point of enlisting over one thousand groups of carolers who bring cheer to state and private institutions and hospitals as well as to residential neighborhoods. In recent years they have received more than $50,000 to contribute to seventy-five child-welfare agencies. The organization has functioned so admirably that inquiries are received over and over from other cities concerning the plan.

Christmas Cards

While Christmas cards are one of the major elements in the observance of the season, some one and a half billion being sent annually, or an average of about sixty per family, the custom is comparatively new. The exact year of its beginning may never be established, but it seems clear that it was in the decade of the 1840's that the first cards were produced. George Buday states, in his *The Story of the Christmas Card*, that the Cole-Horsley Card, which has received considerable attention, appeared in 1843. This was a card made for Sir Henry Cole by John Calcott Horsley, portraying "brimming cheer" in the center, and at each side of the happy family group, in smaller panels, were shown acts of charity — " Feeding the Hungry " and " Clothing the Naked." A thousand of these were lithographed by a Mr. Jobbins of Warwick Court, Holborn, and sold by a gift-book company in Old Bond Street for a shilling apiece.

A vicar of Newcastle, the Rev. Edward Bradley, is reported to have sent lithographed holiday greetings to his friends in 1844. An artist of the Royal Academy in London, W. A. Dobson, sent out hand-colored cards in 1844. William Egley, son of a painter of miniatures, produced a card in 1842 or 1849, depending on the way the last figure in the date on the card is interpreted. If the authority on women's dress, who claims the costumes on the Egley card are more like the styles of 1842 than those of 1849, is correct, then this card would receive the honor of having been the earliest.

Clearer than the date of its origin is the fact that the Christmas-card idea had its beginning in England and gained ground there rapidly — especially in the 1860's when new processes of color printing lowered the cost. Today there are wide selections of religious and secular, highly artistic and homemade types, with individualized messages for doctors, teachers, ministers, servicemen, for baby's first Christmas, and many others. Though it has become big business and though it requires thousands of extra mailmen in December, the Christmas card does bring much " joy to the world " and can be a means of expressing good will to those with whom we cannot correspond oftener than once a year.

Christmas Seals

Slightly newer than the Christmas card is the Christmas seal. Of its origin we can speak with greater certainty, since it is undisputed that a postal clerk, Einar Holboell, born in Denmark in 1865, ordered the first Christmas seals printed and sold at regular post offices in Denmark. While stamping letters and Christmas cards in 1903 in the post office at Copenhagen, the idea occurred to him, Why not have a special Christmas stamp printed for the many tuberculosis sufferers who need hospital treatment? The first year more than four million stamps were sold, yielding some $18,000. Sweden adopted the plan the same year and Norway two years later.

Strange to say, the introduction of the idea into the United States was much slower. Jacob Riis, the noted New York social worker, wrote an article " The Christmas Stamp " for *The Outlook*, July 6, 1907, calling attention to the work in Denmark and reporting that one hundred thousand were dying annually of the disease in our country. The movement for adopting the stamp was strengthened greatly through the efforts of Miss Emily Bissell of Wilmington, Delaware, State Secretary of the Red Cross. Spurred on by the need of $300 to keep the local tuberculosis institution functioning, she designed the first Christmas seal herself. It had a half wreath of holly and a cross, with "Merry Christmas" in the center and "Happy New Year" at the bottom.

She had them printed by a kindhearted printer, and the first stamps were put on sale at the Wilmington, Delaware, post office. But the seals sold slowly. Only through persistent promotion by the editor of the Philadelphia *North American* and endorsement by such national leaders as Theodore Roosevelt and the Chief Justice of the Supreme Court did the seals produce enough money to keep the sanitarium open.

After Miss Bissell won the support of the Red Cross, the sales increased in 1908 to $135,000, and since that time substantial sums have been raised through this simple device.

At present more than three thousand organizations are affiliated with the National Tuberculosis Association. The disease has dropped from first to seventh as a cause of death in this country — from 180.6 per thousand population to 26. Forty-five countries now sell such seals, and the stamp idea has been adapted to Easter Seals for crippled children, and also to many private institutions and organizations, notable among the latter being the American Bible Society.

Since 1919 the double-barred Cross of Lorraine (the Standard of Godfrey of Lorraine, leader of the First Crusade) has served as a permanent emblem for the Christmas seal, though each year a new design is selected for the stamp. Noted artists have contributed their talent, and collectors value early issues so highly that good prices are being paid, especially for the 1911 edition made for vending machines.

While great progress has been made against tuberculosis, both as to prevention and treatment, it still claims some fifty thousand victims each year. The need continues to "lick the foe by licking stamps" and sending out "Christmas voices" for better health.

The Christmas Stocking

The custom immortalized in "Hang up the baby's stocking" is said to have originated with the legend associated with

Bishop Nicholas at the time he generously provided dowries for the three daughters of a nobleman who had lost his fortune in unsuccessful business ventures. As the saint threw each one of the purses, or bags, of gold into the house, it fell into a stocking that had been hung near the chimney to dry.

A variation of the idea appears in Holland, where the children set their shoes in the chimney corners on the eve of December 6, awaiting presents before the next morning. Possibly the greatest impetus to the stocking custom was given by the vivid portrayal in Clement C. Moore's " A Visit from St. Nicholas."

Gifts or Exchanging Presents?

" God so loved the world that he gave . . ." " Thanks be unto God for his unspeakable gift." The Wise Men bowed before the Holy Babe and presented him with gold, frankincense, and myrrh.

In these few lines we have the pure, unalloyed spirit of Christmas-giving which should and frequently does characterize the Nativity season. Giving to shut-ins, to inmates of hospitals and other institutions, to servicemen away from home — these and many more are expressions of unselfish giving.

Boxing Day, while no longer observed commonly under that name, is with us in another form. Centuries ago it was customary in England on December 26 to give Christmas boxes to servants and those who performed public services — to tradesmen, mailmen, police, street sweepers, milkmen, cabmen, newsboys, and the like. Most of us recognize all these and others in modern form. Is it not common for employers to be confronted by not merely expectations of but demands for a Christmas bonus?

But there is a third kind of giving that should be clearly distinguished from the above — the exchange of presents. While it, no doubt, constitutes the great bulk of Christmas merchandising (the Christmas trade being estimated at fourteen billion in 1950), it can, rightly used, be the means of establishing cordial, warm relationships in families and among friends.

The Sheaf of Grain

In Scandinavian countries as well as in Scandinavian settlements in the New World, a sheaf of grain is attached to a pole and placed outside in the snow-covered yards as a Christmas feast for the birds. Often suet is tied to the trees as an extra treat. It is said that no peasant will sit down to his Christmas meal until this ample provision has been made for his feathered friends.

While this is a splendid custom to encourage in rural areas, it is well not to forget that the birds in the cities may be equally appreciative of whatever food may be provided for them, all the way from scraps and crumbs from the table to well-designed bird feeders filled with grain obtained at any feed store.

The Wassail Bowl

The word "wassail" is derived from the Anglo-Saxon *waes hael*, which meant "Be in health" or "Here's to you." Wassail was a mixture of mulled ale, eggs, curdled cream, roasted apples, nuts, and spices.

The custom of serving wassail originated, tradition tells us, with the beautiful Saxon maiden, Rowena, presenting Prince Vortigen with a bowl of wine and greeting him with "*Waes hael*." Gradually much pomp developed around wassail-drinking, the carrying in of the great bowl, the singing of a carol praising the drink, and finally the crowding around for a taste of the steaming mixture.

While the wassail bowl has not disappeared, it has been very largely supplanted by caroling, even as indicated in the song "Here We Come A-Wassailing" being also sung as "A-Caroling."

CHRISTMAS FACTS AND FANCIES

A "Merry Christmas" in Thirty-three Languages

Afrikander . . . . Een Plesierige Kerfees
Argentine . Felices Pasquas Y Felices Ano Nuevo

Bohemian .... Vesele Vanoce
Brazilian .... Boas Festas e Feliz Ano Novo
Bulgarian .... Chestita Koleda
Chinese .. Kung Hsi Hsin Nien bing Chu Shen
      Tan
Croatian .... Sretan Bozic
Danish .... Glædelig Jul
English .... Merry Christmas
Esperanto .... Gajan Kristnaskon
Esthonian .... Roomsaid Joulu Puhi
Finnish .... Houska Joulua
French .... Joyeux Noël
German .... Froehliche Weihnachten
Holland .. Vrolyk Kerstfeest en Gelukkig Nieuw
      Jaar
Hungarian ..... Kellemes Karacsonyi unnepeket
Iraqian .... Idah Saidan Wa Sanah Jadidah
Irish .... Nodlaig mhaith chugnat
Italian .... Buone Feste Natalizie
Jugoslavian .... Cestitamo Bozic
Lettish .... Priecigus Ziemassvetkus
Lithuanian .... Linksmu Kaledu
Norwegian .... God Jul Og Godt Nytt Aar
Polish .... Boze Narodzenie
Portuguese .... Boas Festas
Rumanian .... Sarbatori vesele
Serbian .... Hristos se rodi
Slovakian .... Sretan Bozic or Vesele vianoce
Spanish .... Feliz Navidad
Swedish .. God Jul and (Och) Ett Gott Nytt Ar
Turkish .. Noeliniz Ve Yeni Yiliniz Kutlu Olsun
Ukrainian .... Srozhdestvom Kristovym
Welsh .... Nadolig Llawen

Christmas Greetings in Six Languages

On Christmas, when old friends are meeting,
We give that long-loved joyous greeting —
    " Merry Christmas! "

While hanging sheaves for winter birds
Friends in Norway call the words,
　　　" Gloedelig Jul! "

With wooden shoes ranged on the hearth,
Dutch celebrators cry their mirth,
　　　" Een prettiga Kertmis! "

In France, that land of courtesy,
Our welcome to our guests would be,
　　　" Joyeux Noël! "

Enshrining Christmas in her art,
Italy cries from a full heart,
　　　" Buon Natale! "

When in the land of Christmas trees,
Old Germany, use words like these —
　　　" Froehliche Weihnachten! "

Though each land names a different name,
Good will rings through each wish the same —
　　　" Merry Christmas! "
　　　　　— Dorothy Brown Thompson

" Christmas " Towns

Five communities in the United States and one in Canada
are named for the Nativity season:

Christmas, Gila County, Arizona
Christmas, Orange County, Florida
Christmas, Lawrence County, Kentucky
Christmas, Bolivar County, Mississippi
Christmas, Roane County, Tennessee
Christmas Island, Nova Scotia

In addition, Minnesota, " The Land of Lakes," prides itself on
having a lake in Scott County by the name of Christmas.

A few facts about Christmas, Orange County, Florida, as typical, may be of interest. It is a town of 250 people, near Orlando. As a fort it was completed on Christmas, 1835, and so received its name. Connected with the other states by the United States mail, the post office has been kept busy throughout December remailing cards, letters, and packages. In one year it handled over 300,000 pieces of mail. Lately a permanent Christmas tree with weatherproof ornaments has been erected.

A " Christmas " Village

Torrington, Connecticut, erects for its children in December a Christmas village, where Santa and his elves work on toys, surrounded by shelves loaded with gifts. Santa chats with the youngsters and provides each one with a gift.

His sleigh and reindeer are likewise an attraction and include Rudolph, the Red-nosed Reindeer. The Nativity scene with the Holy Family is lighted by a Star of Bethlehem.

The Poinsettia

While the poinsettia has no Christmas tradition nor special symbolism, its beautiful red and green leaves and yellow center have caused it to become a favorite decoration and it is inseparably associated with Christmas. While native to Central America and Mexico, it has been adapted to our country by Dr. Joel R. Poinsett, of Charleston, South Carolina, and has gained rapid acceptance.

Saint Nicholas — Name Variations

While the saint of Myra continues to be known historically as Saint Nicholas, it is interesting to observe the variations, even the corruptions, that the name has been subject to, most of them easily identifiable. In different countries he is known as *Sankt Nikolaus, Sint Nicolaas, Santa Klaas, Father Christmas, Père Noël, Befana,* and *Kriss Kringle* — the latter more likely a corruption of the German *Krist Kindlein*. But whatever the form of the name, he has become a symbol of unselfish generosity, good cheer, and joy.

Santa Claus, Indiana

Two explanations have arisen for naming this small town near Evansville, Indiana, after the modified name of Saint Nicholas. About seventy-five years ago this town applied for a post office and suggested the name of Santa Fe. When it was learned that this name already applied to a post office in the state, the people decided to name it Santaclause, changing it in 1928 to the customary two words.

A second version says that in 1882, on Christmas Eve, while some residents were discussing in the general store the naming of their town, Santa Claus walked in. Unanimously they called out, " Let's name it Santa Claus."

Whichever explanation is correct, the town has been busy both summer and winter in recent years. In summer, tourists stop in to see the museum, the original post office with its fine collection of toys of the past decades. A Santa Claus Park, life-size Mother Goose figures, Kriss Kringle Street, and a colored statue of the white-bearded saint, twenty-three feet high, weighing forty-two tons — all these make it a rare attraction during the ten months when Christmas mail is of secondary interest.

In November and December some sixty thousand pieces a day frequently pass through the post office — some three million pieces in a single season. Whereas formerly letters addressed to Saint Nick had to be destroyed because of lack of help, since 1938 the local American Legion Post offered to answer them, at times receiving assistance from posts in other localities in investigating worthy requests.

Santa's Workshop — North Pole

Another village, pervaded by the same spirit but assuming a somewhat different form, is Santa's Workshop, or North Pole, located on the side of Whiteface Mountain at Wilmington, New York, near Lake Placid. Completed in 1949, the ten log houses with steep roofs, a permanent home for Santa Claus, a post office, a blacksmith shop, and a small chapel with an attractive Nativity scene were designed by Arto Monaco. He had worked formerly with Walt Disney.

It is truly Santa's workshop, since in several of the buildings he and his assistants are busy making toys and gifts. For added realism the North Pole finds a place for live reindeer, ponies, sheep, and goats as part of the village.

The workshop is open from June 1 to November 1 and has attracted over a quarter of a million people in less than a decade.

2. Christmas in Europe

RATHER than begin with our own Christmas customs and view those of other lands later, it seems more logical and helpful to acquaint ourselves with those of Europe first, since it is to that continent that we are most directly indebted for so much of what has become an almost indistinguishable part of our culture.

For the sake of convenience, in referring to the various countries and peoples, we turn alphabetically to the countries of Europe first.

Austria

Christmas (both December 25 and 26 are legal holidays) is Austria's most important holiday of the year. This country's contribution of the world's most beloved song " Silent Night! Holy Night! " makes us all deeply indebted to these noble people.

While the American Santa Claus is not known in Austria, he appears in another form on December 6, a day honoring the patron saint of children. Saint Nicholas (*Santaklausen*) makes his appearance, accompanied by the devil. The children must give both of them information about their good deeds and bad deeds.

When the devil prepares to strike with a rod, Saint Nicholas chases the children away. When the children promise to be good, he gives them nuts, fruit, and candy.

On Christmas Eve, after a dinner of fried carp, the family gathers around the fir or pine tree, which the parents have decorated with candles, cookies, and other ornaments. The presents are spread out around the tree, but the center of attraction is the manger scene, consisting of as many as one hundred units, carefully preserved from year to year.

At midnight, Christmas matins are celebrated in all Austrian churches, the peasants generally coming down the mountains with lighted torches in their hands. On December 25 and 26 families and friends visit one another and enjoy roast goose, ham, and special Christmas sweets, including rich fruitcake.

Quite widespread are the Nativity plays dealing with the flight of the Holy Family to Egypt, the birth of Christ, the stories of the shepherds and the Wise Men.

"Turmblasen" is a traditional feature of Christmas Eve, brass instruments playing chorale music from the city tower or the steeple of the main church.

"Showing the Christ-child" consists of carrying a manger from house to house and singing carols along the way. In the mountain villages a custom prevails in which the family living farthest from the church start out with torches, caroling, toward the neighbor's home. Family after family join until they gather on the steps of the church. After they have sung and acted out "Through the darkness gleams the light," the final chorus is sung by the whole village, triumphant in their faith and certainty, "Christ the Savior is born."

Belgium

In Belgium all look forward to the Christmas procession, which winds its way through the streets. In Antwerp the bells all over the city are ringing, and loudest of all are those of the cathedral. Bands, children singing, priests chanting — all take their places in the procession — and last of all the Cardinal, clad in gorgeous color. When the procession is over, the people crowd into the church. This service is followed by a home celebration with candles and songs.

To the people in that romantic corner of Belgium, called Flanders, the coming of Christmas means extensive preparations for the traditional Christmas plays. In each of the churches, the congregation presents a Christmas play, and the people take great pride in their production. Each of the leading characters is selected with great care and instructed to perform his part with accuracy and decorum. As a general rule the children of the school are selected to portray the angels. Their main activity consists in chorusing the " Gloria in Excelsis " with their youthful soprano voices. Changes are introduced on an individual basis in accordance with the whims of the people in each town. For this reason some of the casts include some rather unusual characters.

In some of the border towns where smuggling is a rather common occurrence, the cast of characters will include a poacher or smuggler, who also brings his gift to the Christ-child. This is reminiscent of the fact that Christ came to this world to save all people, even the sinners, and that no one need fear Christ.

One of the requirements for all the Nativity plays in Flanders is that each character who participates must resemble some character from one of Brueghel's paintings. This limits the use of costumes to those which were worn by the ordinary townspeople back in the sixteenth century when Brueghel did his painting. With such costumes it is natural that much of the dramatic acting that was characteristic of the sixteenth-century Nativity plays has also been retained.

It is also a Christmas custom for each village in Flanders to appoint three men who have the privilege of walking along the streets dressed as the Magi. In order to receive this appointment the men must have been outstanding for their practice of virtue during the preceding year. Attired in their robes, they make their rounds and sing two songs at the door of each home in town. One song describes the journey of the Magi. The other is the Flemish version of " O Tannenbaum." At the end of their two songs the Magi are usually invited in for a cup of tea or some pancakes. It takes a hardy trio to keep up with the demands made on their appetites and their capacities. Yet, this is Christmas to Flanders, where old traditions survive.

Bulgaria

In Bulgaria a quaint ceremony begins on Christmas Day. Before breakfast some corn is placed in a stocking, and the head of the house sprinkles a portion of it on the doorstep, saying, " Christ is born," to which the family responds, " He is born indeed." Then the man approaches the fireplace and strikes the blazing log, and with each blow he utters a wish of good health to the stock, to the land, and a wish for a bountiful harvest. Then the ashes of the log are carefully gathered, a coin is hidden in them, and pieces of the ends are placed in trees to assure a good crop.

Czechoslovakia

Christmas observances in this country, formerly Bohemia and Poland, begin with *Svatej Nikulas* Day, December 6, and end with the visit of the *Tri Kralu* (Three Kings), January 6. On December 6, Saint Nicholas is supposed to come down from the sky, with an angel carrying a bag of gifts for the good and leading the devil who carries switches for the naughty ones. As soon as the children hear them coming, they rush to the table and say their prayers. If they know their prayers well, they are rewarded.

With this excitement over, Christmas preparations are begun in earnest. The children are promised that if they fast faithfully, they will see the golden pigs at suppertime. At the beginning of the supper, the family exchange greetings, starting with the oldest and ending with the youngest. The candles are lighted, and lo, the pigs appear on the wall and ceiling, the flickering of the lighted candles performing the trick, since at the center of the table is the young pig, a part of the sumptuous meal. One chair at the table is left vacant for the Christ-child.

At midnight all get ready for church, for the holy mass called *Pasterka*. On Christmas Day the churches are decorated with evergreens and Christmas trees. The manger, the *jeslicky*, is never missing in the church and seldom in the home. The celebration continues for three days.

France

While not a legal holiday, Saint Nicholas Day, December 6, is observed quite generally in eastern France, where it has gradually replaced Christmas as regards the giving of candy and gifts to the children. As in neighboring European countries, the good children receive toys and the bad ones are scolded.

Christmas Day is celebrated by religious services and family dinners. During the weeks preceding, the shop windows of the big Parisian department stores contain fabulous displays of animated figures.

Family celebrations begin with the decoration of the tree a few days before Christmas. Candles, tinsel, and many-colored stars are used. On Christmas Eve, when the children are asleep, little toys, candies, and fruits are hung on the branches to add to the gifts that Father Christmas (*Père Noël*) has left in their shoes before the fireplace.

The manger contains small figurines including representations of Jesus, Mary, and Joseph, the cow, the donkey, and the shepherds. In some regions little, painted clay figures called *santons* (little saints) are used, representing not only the Biblical characters but also the people of everyday life — the mayor, priest, policeman, butcher, baker, and others. The capital of the world for *santons* is the little town of Aubagne. Although the crèche was introduced by Francis of Assisi in 1224, it was not until the sixteenth century that the making of crèches became widespread.

At midnight three masses are held for which the churches and the cathedrals are beautifully lighted and echo forth the joyful melodies of carols, bells, and carillons.

When the family returns home, there is a supper known as *le reveillon.* This may consist of baked ham, roast fowl, salads, cake, fruit, bonbons, and wine, but it varies from region to region. In Alsace, for example, the traditional goose is given the place of honor on the table. The Bretons serve buckwheat cakes with sour cream. Turkey and chestnuts are served in Burgundy. The favorite dish of Paris and the Il-de-France region is oysters, and the cake is in the form of a yule log. In Paris, as might be expected, dancing, champagne, and dining are more prominent, while the religious note prevails more in outlying regions.

In the morning the children get up all excited to see the gifts at the hearth and on the tree. The whole family gathers for the exchange of gifts.

From the combination of the first mangers and of the earliest carols came the liturgical drama given in the cathedral squares at Christmas. From the fourteenth century onward, the story of Christ's birth has been given in the form of "mysteries of the Nativity" and also in puppet plays.

Germany

Germany is the land of Christmas trees and of Christmas toys. In no other country is the day so fully and heartily observed. From the eve of December 6, stores, markets, and bazaars present a festive appearance. The custom of making something for those you love best has not died out completely. A soap rose, an artificial flower, an embroidered sofa cushion — these are a few things that women and children delight in.

Christmas is a personal and a family affair for which preparations begin weeks ahead. Advent wreaths and Advent candles call attention to the season, beginning with the fourth Sunday preceding the festive day. Some ten million households require one or two trees. Usually the mother does the trimming and provides the table for the gifts, not admitting anyone else into the room. At six o'clock Christmas Eve the family views the tree decorated with shiny tinsel, bright-colored balls, and cookies baked in the shape of men, women, animals, stars, hearts, and the like.

The children receive their gifts through the *Christkind*, often represented as dressed in white robes, wearing a golden crown, and having big golden wings. Saint Nicholas goes about observing the children's behavior and leaves bundles of rods where needed. In some places Knecht Ruprecht takes his place in visiting the houses but not to the exclusion of Kriss Kringle (corruption of *Christkind*), since the German children seldom forget that the gifts come through the Christ-child, and that the season is not for selfish enjoyment but to bring joy to others and to have a concern for the less fortunate.

Many churches are open during the entire week before Christmas. Though they are not trimmed in the manner we are accustomed to, the people listen with devotion to the retelling of the story of that first Holy Night, often on Christmas Eve, regularly on December 25, and a large number once more on the second Christmas Day.

Great Britain

England has probably celebrated the merriest of yuletides. In feudal times the castle halls resounded with feasting and merrymaking. It is the land of the yule log, the plum pudding, the boar's head, the Christmas carol, and the Christmas card. While few fireplaces are big enough today to accommodate a typical yule log and the boar's head ceremony has lost some of its former appeal, the season continues to be one of religious services, family reunions, and of merrymaking.

Carol-singing at home and at church is gaining in favor. The custom of sending greeting cards, begun in the 1840's, continues to expand. In recent years the Christmas message of the Queen, broadcast to all parts of the British Commonwealth on Christmas Day, continues a tradition begun by King George V. Another recent innovation is the erection of a huge, gaily decorated Christmas tree in Trafalgar Square, an annual presentation by the city of Oslo to commemorate Anglo-Norwegian co-operation during World War II.

On Christmas Eve the children hang up their stockings above the fireplace or at their beds so that Father Christmas can fill them. The parents decorate the tree after the children have gone to bed, and the houses are decorated with holly, mistletoe, and gay paper chains and streamers. At midnight church services often feature carol-singing. Frequently special Christmas services are held the next day.

Christmas dinner is usually served in the early afternoon and includes turkey, roast potatoes, mince pie, plum pudding decorated with holly and flaming with brandy. The dinner is finished with candies, nuts, and fruits. In the late afternoon or early evening, tea is served accompanied by a rich fruitcake with a thick almond-paste icing.

Ireland and *Scotland* enjoy similar Christmas cheer but on a less lavish scale. The Irish place lighted candles in their windows on Christmas Eve as a guide and an invitation to all, who, like Mary and Joseph, may be looking for shelter. Wanderers are given a good meal and lodging and sent on their way in the morning with a few coins in their pockets.

> On Christmas Eve a candlelight
> To shine abroad through Christmas night,
> That those who pass may see its glow,
> And walk with Christ a mile or so.

Another Irish holiday feature is " Feeding the Wren." For a time a wren was killed and carried from door to door by the wren boys, who sang songs and expected money in return. Lately a more humane practice has superseded it. A wren is caught and after placing it in a cage, it is perched on top of a bush. Then money is solicited avowedly for the starving wren.

In *Scotland* the main celebrations and family reunions are reserved for New Year's Eve and New Year's Day. It is at this time that shortbread, black buns, a very rich fruit-and-nut cake heavily spiced, form the menu.

In *Wales* carol-singing is possibly even more firmly established than in England. Songs are sung to the harp in the church for the early morning service, in the homes of the people, and at the doors of the houses. With its several choirs of carolers in almost every village, these music-loving people gather in the public square to learn who, during the year, has won the prize for submitting the best music for a new carol and the formal adoption of it as the carol of the year. Thus a new carol is added each year to the carolers' favorites.

The Christmas goose is an institution, and so popular is taffy-making in this season that "without it the inhabitants would not know that Christmas had come."

Greece

Although Easter is the main holiday in Greece, being regarded as more significant by the church, Christmas is also a period of considerable celebration. On Christmas Eve, before the family goes to mass, the boys gather in groups to sing carols in front of the houses, accompanied by the beating of small drums and the tinkling of steel triangles. Generally they are rewarded with dried figs, walnuts, almonds, cookies, and in the towns, with money.

After the return from mass (it begins at 4:00 A.M. and ends shortly before daybreak), the family board is laden with Christmas treats. Not only are nuts, oranges, tangerines, and pomegranates popular but likewise *Christpsomo* (bread of Christ) and *Kourabiedes*. The former is a simple cake decorated with nuts. The latter are small cakes covered with powdered sugar, which, when soaked in diluted honey, are called *melomacaroma*.

There are no Christmas trees and no presents. The presents come on Saint Basil's Day (one of the four Fathers of the Orthodox Church, born in Caesarea, in Asia Minor, 330).

A superstitious practice of throwing a little cross into the water on Epiphany brings the festive season to a close. The *Kalli-kantzari* (gremlin-like spirits) are, through the priest's act, supposed to rush headlong back to their haunts. To make sure that none lurks in forgotten corners, the village priest goes from house to house sprinkling holy water everywhere to bless the home. In America the best-known ceremonies of the blessing of the water are at Tarpon Springs, Florida, and at Asbury Park, New Jersey.

Holland

In Holland, Saint Nicholas Day, December 6, has remained the great day for the children. It seems that the honored saint is at home here more than in any other country. Holland, with its long coast line, its wide rivers and seafaring population, counts no less than twenty-three Saint Nicholas churches.

On the last Saturday in November the words, " Look, there is the steamer bringing us Saint Nick! " are acted out, and for the last twenty-five years the words of the song " Here Comes Saint Nicholas! " have been taken literally.

> Look, there is the steamer from faraway lands,
> It brings us Saint Nicholas; he's waving his hands.
> His horse is a-prancing on deck up and down,
> The banners are waving in village and town.
>
> Black Peter is laughing and tells every one,
> " The good kids get candy, the bad ones get none! "
> Oh, please, dear Saint Nicholas, if Pete and you would
> Just visit our house, for we all have been good.

Accordingly, Saint Nicholas, wearing a bishop's robe and miter, white gloves, and an enormous bishop's ring on his left hand, seated on his white horse and accompanied by Black Peter (the name given to the devil for this occasion), arrives by steamer in Amsterdam's harbor and in other harbor cities, cheered by thousands of children and adults, and majestically descends the gangplank. Peter, in the puffed velvet breeches and the plumed beret of sixteenth-century Spain, a sack on his shoulder, and a birch rod in his hand, hovers around to see that all is well with his beloved master.

Amid deafening cheers and with all the church bells ringing, the parade is set in motion. First come a motorcade of the police force and a brass band. Then comes Saint Nick on horseback, wrapped in his scarlet mantle, with Black Peter at his side. The mayor and other city dignitaries follow, decorated floats, a cavalcade of students, and more brass bands. The procession stops in the main square in Amsterdam, in front of the Royal Palace, to be welcomed by the Queen.

Saint Nicholas parties are most commonly planned for Christmas Eve. Inexpensive gifts, each accompanied by a verse and elaborately and mysteriously wrapped, are provided for all. When the presents have all been distributed, the children are packed to bed, and the older people partake of tea and hard cookies (*speculaas*) until their own surprises begin to arrive. At ten o'clock the room is cleared, and *letterbanket* (cakes made in the form of an initial) and hot punch or milk chocolate are provided. Finally a dish of boiled chestnuts, steaming hot, is brought in, and chestnuts are eaten with butter and salt.

Christmas Day is celebrated in an atmosphere of serenity and good will. There is a tree, of course. The houses are decorated with pine and holly, and special foods are served. But the gayer parties and presents have been a part of the Saint Nicholas Eve celebrations.

A part of Christmas Eve or Christmas morning is devoted to churchgoing; the afternoon is spent in the family circle, and at seven an abundant dinner is served. On the second Christmas Day practically all Dutch music societies, radio ensembles, professional vocalists, school choirs, and amateur groups take part in some performance or other in churches, concert halls, and other available auditoriums. It is as if the Dutch singing voice were suddenly bursting forth to greet the coming of the Savior.

Hungary

As in several other European countries, Saint Nicholas, in bishop's robes, goes about December 6 and distributes rewards to good children and admonitions to naughty ones. Usually the children place their boots or shoes on the window sills so that Saint Nick may leave small gifts or birch rods in them.

Christmas in Hungary lasts two days. Christmas Eve is an occasion for festivity. Before the evening meal, the family assembles around a Christmas tree, and after a short prayer, gifts are distributed. When the first star appears, the evening meal is served. Carol-singing and church services on both the first and second Christmas days are so real a part of the festive season that the Hungarian Americans continue to give the church this same large place in the observance of the anniversary of Christ's birth.

Italy

Three weeks constitute the Christmas season in Italy — from the beginning of the novena (eight days preceding Christmas) until after Twelfth-night, or the Feast of Epiphany. During the novena, children go from place to place reciting Christmas selections and expecting coins with which to purchase special delicacies of the season. In some provinces shepherds go from house to house and, if welcomed, leave a wooden spoon to mark the place and then later bring their musical instruments to play and sing Christmas songs.

All the families that can possibly afford a *presepio*, a miniature representation of the Holy Family and the manger, center their Christmas around that. Guests kneel in front of it, musicians sing before it; around it at early twilight on Christmas Eve candles are lighted, and the little folks recite their poems.

While a rigid fast is observed the twenty-four hours preceding Christmas Eve, it is followed by as elaborate a banquet as can be afforded. Thereupon follows the drawing of presents from the " Urn of Fate." Though many blanks are included, and these merely add to the merriment, ultimately a present for each one is provided. At sunset the booming of cannon from the Castle of St. Angelo in Rome proclaims the opening of the Holy Season. By nine o'clock all, young and old, repair to the churches to behold the procession of church officials in their beautiful robes and to participate in the celebration of the mass.

Each church seeks to exhibit the biggest or the most artistic manger (*presepio*). The most beautiful is that of the Ara Coeli Church in Rome. From a high platform erected in front of the *presepio*, Roman children like to deliver little sermons, recite poems, and tell the story of *Gesu Bambino*.

Gifts are brought by the Christ-child. The actual season for a large-scale exchange of gifts is not Christmas but the day of Epiphany (January 6) when the *Befana* (a corruption of *Epiphania*) is the benefactress. She is represented as a benevolent witch coming down the chimney filling the children's shoes with goodies, or at times with a few pieces of charcoal!

Cities and villages have the usual festive decorations and window displays. Typical among these is Rome's historic Piazza Navona, with the huge *presepio*, its innumerable stands selling crib figurines as well as Christmas sweets, the movement of shoppers and strollers, the shouts of the vendors, and the tunes of the bagpipers mingling in a carnival of merriment.

Lithuania

Lithuanians cover their Christmas Eve dinner table with layers of straw in memory of the night in Bethlehem. An unconsecrated wafer, symbolizing the love, harmony, and good will of the season, is shared by all the members of the family.

Rumania

Christmas festivities in Rumania begin on the twenty-fourth of December. In every household a special kind of cake, called *turte*, is eaten. It is made of many layers of thin dough, with melted sugar or honey and crushed walnuts. While preparing the dough, the housewife takes some of it for a superstitious tree ceremony. The husband follows her and as they approach a tree, he threatens to cut it down with an ax, saying, " This tree is useless; it bears no fruit." But the woman speaks up to save the tree, saying, " I am sure it will be as full of fruit next summer as my hands are full of dough." In this manner they seek to coax the trees into fruit-bearing!

Boys pass from house to house repeating the familiar greetings and carrying long bags into which they pack the gifts offered them. They begin singing the greetings, called *colinde*, on the evening of the twenty-fourth and at New Year's change their verses appropriately. The *colinde* are sung at night. During the daytime a star called the *steaua* is used. It is placed on a pole, and little bells under it announce the approach of the singers.

The shepherds who live in cottages throughout the valleys and among the hills gather at Christmas time to go from place to place to enact a play based on the Slaughter of the Innocents, the principal characters being Herod, the Magi, an angel, a child, and two Roman soldiers. Without costumes or scenery they perform in a sincere and impressive manner.

At Epiphany the priest goes to the homes of his parishioners and blesses them. He dips a bunch of basil in holy water and sprinkles the houses with it. He carries with him a kettle in which the people drop coins and gifts of ham, hemp, and grain. With the hemp the priests often make their own cloth, and the food goes toward their support.

Russia (Old Russia)

In a country that covers one sixth of the land surface of the globe, customs naturally vary, and since the Revolution but little of the old remains. Of the typical yuletide observances of the country, the *Kolyada* (Father Christmas) songs are most common. They were sacrificial songs in heathen days, covering a variety of themes relating to the gods and goddesses, but have been given such Christian characteristics that they later became the sacred songs of yuletide.

> Kolyada, Kolyada
> Walks about on Christmas Eve;
> Kolyada, Kolyada
> At the window, cakes to leave.

> Kolyada, Kolyada
> Come this holy night we pray;
> Kolyada, Kolyada
> Came and brought us Christmas day.

On Christmas Eve it is customary to fast until after the first service in the church, which means generally the Eastern Orthodox, though there are many other smaller religious groups also. Quite frequently the ceremony of blessing the house and the household is observed. The priest visits the home, accompanied by boys carrying a vessel of holy water, and sprinkles a little in each room.

Christmas trees are quite common, but they have lately been called New Year trees. A brightly lighted revolving tree, seventy-five feet tall, touches the chandeliers of St. George's Hall in the Grand Kremlin Palace.

Santa Claus reigns for the kiddies, but he is called Grandfather Frost. Despite such widespread observances, the celebrations lack the flavor of pre-Revolution days when children trudged through the snow from house to house singing carols, and when every village had its snow games and sleighing parties.

Scandinavia

In the Scandinavian countries — Denmark, Norway, and Sweden — Christmas is so cherished and celebrated that the saying has arisen, " Christmas lasts a month." What has given rise to this exaggerated statement is that the yule celebration does begin quite generally on the thirteenth of December, Saint Lucia's Day, and continues until the thirteenth of January, Saint Knut's Day (also spelled Canute, Cnut, or Knud).

While customs vary as to details in the various countries and from district to district within the larger ones especially, common to all of them is the thorough house cleaning, the abundance of festive cooking and baking, and in Finland a visit to the famous Finnish steam bath preceding Christmas Eve.

Saint Lucia's Day, December 13, opens the season with a colorful festival in which old and new blend harmoniously. Lucia was a Christian maiden martyred during the time of Emperor Diocletian. The story of her death was carried to Sweden, where the Christianized Vikings heard of her. They imagined her shining figure, crowned by a halo of light. Since her saint's day happened to fall on December 13, when daylight soon will increase after the dark winter months, she became even more of a favorite with the people of the north. Today the Day of Saint Lucia, or Lucy, is celebrated all over Sweden, in the cities, out in the country, even in factories and offices. Primarily, though, it is a family observance. Early in the dark morning, in hundreds of thousands of Swedish homes, the members of the family are awakened by the young daughter of the house, who serves them coffee and newly baked Lucia buns and cakes in bed. She is attired in a white, flowing gown, and on her head she wears a wreath of greenery in which are stuck lighted candles. The song she sings, "Santa Lucia," is an old Italian melody that still lingers in the north.

Following Saint Lucia's Day, presents are bought or homemade ones provided, special foods are prepared, and by December 24 all have been temptingly wrapped and the tree is shimmering with ornaments, colorful gifts, and live candles. The sheaf of grain has been placed on top of a pole or tree in order that the birds too may rejoice. By lunch time the streets seem to become emptier, as everyone hastens to his home and the family midday meal. Old and young now gather in the kitchen, which has been decorated with colored candlesticks and vases with flowers and fresh pine branches. On the stove a large iron pot simmers with the drippings of pork, sausage, and corned beef. Slices of wort bread are speared on forks and dipped into the liquid until thoroughly saturated. When the dipping is over, luncheon is served in the dining room.

When this meal is over, dusk is beginning to fall, and frequently the soft, longed-for Christmas snow is falling in gentle flakes outside. The dinner is an intimate and close family gathering, and the menu has been the same for generations and is served in almost every home in Sweden, from north to south. It is usually prefaced by a smörgåsbord. Then comes the fish course, consisting of lutfisk, which generally is sun-cured cod, cunningly prepared and served with a cream sauce This may be followed by a rosy Christmas ham, and the meal is topped off with a white, steaming rice pudding or porridge. In its midst lies an almond hidden, and tradition wants you to believe that he or she who finds it will marry before the next year is up. Nothing is said about persons already married.

The after-dinner coffee is served, followed by almonds, other nuts, candies, and raisins, in the living room, in proximity to the Christmas tree. At last the important moment arrives, when the flickering white candles on the green branches are lighted, and all electric illumination in the room is turned off. A rare and wonderful peace descends, as every eye in quiet contemplation watches the haloed flames. The Christmas spirit has silently stolen into homes and hearts.

After the meal the children await eagerly the presents that have been placed under the tree or are brought in by *Jultomten*, as Kriss Kringle, or Santa Claus, is known in Sweden.

Christmas Day, for centuries, has been mostly a day of rest and of religious observance. The main church event is the pre-dawn service, observed all over Sweden in cities as well as in rural districts. It is, perhaps, most impressive and colorful in the country. Faithful to age-old tradition, the Swedes delight, whenever possible, to drive to church in sleighs. Since the night is still black, the churchgoers in some parts of the country light their way through the snowy, silent forests with flaring torches. Here and there the darkness is pricked by glowing dots, because on Christmas morn almost every house in Sweden has a lighted candle in each window. Between the tall pines and spruce trees lies the country church, the candlelight shining invitingly through the stained-glass windows. Close by the temple, the worshipers toss their torches into a large pile, which flickers in the dark night and casts its reflection on the snow. At the door they are met by the organ notes of a stirring chorale like " How Brightly Beams the Morning Star," and in front of them the altar shines with the radiance of hundreds of burning tapers.

While the first two days of Christmas are largely family affairs, December 26 heralds in the season of hospitality. Children's parties begin in midafternoon, with the grownups taking over in early evening and carrying through until the next morning. In the cities, clubs and civic organizations hold parties for their members, and business firms and factories for their employees. It's a great time for visiting, especially in the rural districts. Great pride is taken in the quality of the food placed before guests at a time like this.

On dark afternoons and early evenings, Scandinavian youngsters dress up in outlandish costumes and go from door to door in small groups, asking for handouts of goodies, very much as American children do on Halloween. This particular tradition is known in Norway as *Julebukk*, or " Christmas buck." To explain why a goat appears at this point, it is necessary to delve far back into the Viking times when the pagan worship of Thor included his goat. In those days a person clad in a goatskin and carrying a goat's head would burst in upon a party of singing and reveling celebrators. During the evening orgy of dancing and singing, the " goat " would pretend to die and then return to life. This pagan yuletide game persisted in the Christian Era when it began to take on a different form. The intruder then appeared dressed as the devil, and as of yore his entry was the signal for boisterous revelry. By the end of the Middle Ages the *Julebukk* custom was forbidden both by the church and the state, but persisted under cover to emerge in more recent times as a rather tame offshoot of the earlier tradition.

On Twelfth-night, youngsters from the villages dress up in strange costumes, often representing some Biblical character. All carry large, transparent paper stars, mounted on poles, with lighted candles inside. They go from house to house, and the hymns and folk songs they sing are so old that many of them are not to be found in any book of music.

Saint Knut's Day, January 13, ends the festive season. The day honors King Knut IV, " the Saint," who ruled 1080–1086. Because of his pious nature, his generosity to the poor, to the churches, and to the priests, and his erection of a magnificent cathedral, he was canonized as a saint and became the patron saint of the brotherhoods or guilds that had been founded in his honor.

Since he had decreed that feasting should prevail during the twenty days of the yuletide celebration, the Christmas tree is lighted for the last time on January 13, the day that honors him. Then it is dismantled and taken outdoors with the wish:

> May God bless your Christmas,
> May it last till Easter.

While parties, visits, and celebrations have continued for some three weeks and the air of festivity continues till the end of January, especially in the rural districts, gradually the work-a-day world reasserts its claims on the celebraters.

Serbia

Early Christmas Eve the father brings in the yule log. Before cutting it down, he crosses himself three times and throws a handful of wheat at the tree, saying, " Happy Christmas Eve to you." In the meantime the boys and girls of the village go from house to house, singing very old songs, and the mothers prepare small cakes in the forms of sheep, pigs, lambs, and chickens. The boys help prepare the Christmas pig to be roasted the next morning.

After sunset the log is ceremoniously lighted, the family joining in the words, " May God and the happy and holy Christmas keep thee." The Christmas Eve supper follows. Fish, beans, cabbage, onions well seasoned with paprika, and plenty of wheat bread make up the meal.

Aside from religious services, the great event on Christmas Day is the roasting of the suckling pig. The family that first succeeds in lighting the courtyard fire and placing the pig before it to roast, fires a pistol to inform the neighbors. Another pistol is fired when the roasting is completed.

Superstitious practices are unfortunately rather common. To have the log stop blazing during the night brings bad luck. Handfuls of wheat are cast about with the prayer for good crops. The log is struck so that thousands of sparks fly up the chimney, with the words, " May we this year have many oxen, many horses, many pigs, many sheep, much honey, all possible good fortune, and happiness in this house."

Possibly the tenderest element in the celebration is the prayer by the father, after which the members of the family kiss each other, saying: " The peace of God be between us today. Christ is born, truly he is born; let us bow before our Christ."

Siberia

In the days when Russia sent its exiles to Siberia, at the time the Christmas dinner was served, the host set aside a portion of every course for " those whom nobody must see," for the escaped prisoners who traveled only by night. Since they had the hearty sympathy of the peasants, every householder aimed to cheer these exiles. So a portion of food was placed on a table just inside a darkened window where the unfortunates could enjoy these few rays of Christmas cheer.

Spain

Here the Christmas season was until recently rigidly observed in the churches, but it was heretofore, and is even more now, characterized by music, mirth, and hilarity, with home and family pleasures occupying a secondary place. Preceding the *Noche Buena*, the good night, the streets in many cities are brilliantly lighted. Plump turkeys, quacking ducks, and cooing pigeons crowd the market places. Delicious fruit, quaint pigskins of wine, booths of toys, shops exhibiting sweets and fancy goods suitable for holiday wear — all these add their part to the festive spirit.

As the stars appear in the heavens, tiny oil lamps are lighted in every house, and among all the devout Roman Catholics the image of the Virgin Mary is illuminated with a taper. In the streets the air is filled with a spirit of unrest and gaiety until the hour of midnight, when the church bells call to midnight mass. It will probably be far into the morning before the crowd turns homeward, for the " wee hours " are spent in singing and dancing. But the Christmas dinner, which is never eaten until after midnight, attracts grandparents, parents, brothers and sisters, aunts and uncles and cousins.

After the feast the family gathers around the Christmas tree which is, perhaps more than any other Christmas custom, typically Protestant, although the idea is rapidly spreading throughout Spain. There they sing the great hymns of Christendom and the Christmas carols so beloved to Christians the world over. The following morning the churches have their services of worship.

Santa Claus, as such, does not visit the little Spanish youngsters, but tradition has it that the three Wise Men never fail to arrive in Spain during the night of the sixth of January, bringing gifts just as they did when they visited Bethlehem many centuries ago. Children place their shoes on the balcony so that the Wise Men will know where to leave their gifts, along with barley, or *cebada*, for the tired camels who must carry their riders through a busy night. Amazingly enough, the children awaken early in the morning to find their shoes overflowing with toys and fruit.

The *Nacimiento*, a representation of Christ's Nativity, attracts the children especially. It is lighted with candles, and the little folks dance around it to the music of tambourines and joyously sing the Nativity songs. At the center is the Babe of Bethlehem, with his devoted parents watching over him. A gray donkey and the typical Spanish bull always look on from the nearby stall. The shepherds and the angel are there, too, on the hillside. Also included is the home of Herod, placed at a distance, and the Wise Men from the East, bearing their precious gifts.

Every Spanish manger scene includes a small stream where women kneel as they tend to the family laundry, so typical of the scene one may find anywhere in Spain. In addition to the innkeeper and numerous animals, there are sometimes figures of well-known *torreros* (bull fighters) and politicians.

In every part of Spain song and dance are the most characteristic features of the yuletide, and they continue until the festivities end on Twelfth-day, Epiphany.

Switzerland

Compared with the Anglo-Saxon Christmas, the Swiss yuletide is a quiet observance. No other festival of the year is so intimately connected with, and restricted to, the family. " Praying before merrymaking " is the rule for this and other religious festivals which all culminate in a " second " holiday. It is Saint Stephen's Day (December 26) at Christmas, and it is Monday at Easter and Monday at Whitsun.

The snow-clad Alpine hills and valleys make Christmas especially romantic in this central European republic. Here the *Christkindli*, the Swiss Santa Claus, in the form of a radiant angel, drives through the village street in a sleigh drawn by six tiny reindeer. On the sleigh are trees and packages of gifts, fruits, and nuts to be distributed with the aid of the helpers.

Before the youngsters are allowed to play with their toys, the family gathers around the tree to sing the familiar carols, and in many a home the story of Bethlehem is read again from the family Bible. As in practically every other country, Christmas Eve services are held.

On Christmas Eve the church bells only are allowed to break the silence. Their powerful chimes call to the midnight church services. The famous bells of Zurich have been trained in harmony for hundreds of years. As they slowly blend into one single symphonic concert, their awe-inspiring sound fills every nook of space in the wide valley from which the city gracefully reaches up to the surrounding hills. The bells of Zurich have carried their message around the world. They have been heard in a great many radio broadcasts and on phonograph records.

In the Valais, one of Switzerland's quaintest mountain cantons, the bell-ringing tradition becomes a bell-ringing competition on Christmas Eve, as it does on the eves of all religious festivals. Each community in each valley wants to show that it has the most beautiful bells and consequently tries to " out-ring " its rivals. After the midnight mass everyone gathers around the family table for a frugal supper consisting of *Ringli* (king-sized doughnuts) and hot chocolate. In the mountain villages of the Valais, the New Year is greeted by groups of singers passing from house to house.

Among the peasants of the mountain regions, the week between Christmas and New Year's is visiting week, and it is a common sight to see two or three generations emerge from the same home, all equipped with skis, and all bound for a *Kaffeeklatsch*, a social evening at some neighbor's. At Zurich, it is reported, children dress in long, white nightshirts and flowing beards; high hats ornamented with lights and trimmings crown each head. Processions are formed, the boys carrying cowbells, potlids, whips, and other noisemakers. From house to house they go, and at each place a simple gift awaits them — just a token of good cheer.

The *Christkindli*, in person, this very symbol of the Holy Night so dear to the Swiss children, still makes a personal appearance in and around the village and castle of Hallwil on the charming lake of the same name. *Christkindli* is personified by a girl in snow-white garb, her little face veiled and her little head crowned with gold and sparkling gems. She is accompanied by children dressed in white, following her on her calls at every house. Baskets full of gifts and colorful lanterns are carried through the village, and the tinkling of a silvery bell announces the heavenly visitor and her companions. As soon as the *Christkindli* enters a house, the Christmas tree is lighted and the gifts find their way into eager hands out of the basket. The *Christkindli* smilingly shakes hands with everyone present while her young attendants sing their carols. And on they go to the neighboring house until all the children in the village have had their date with the Holy Child.

One of the strangest Swiss Christmas cookies is the *Tirggel,* of Zurich, which is said to be derived from an early Germanic sacrificial cake. These golden-brown flat cakes originally featured animal designs as tokens of offerings. Evidence of the pre-Christian origins of the *Tirggel* is shown by its ingredients, which are flour and honey without any addition of sugar. It therefore dates back to an era long before sugar became known in Europe. The artfully carved wooden molds in which the dough is baked have seen many artistic improvements in the course of the centuries. The sacrificial animals have been largely replaced by ornamental, cartoonlike illustrations of the Christmas story and the heroic deeds of William Tell. The *Tirggel*, in its more or less sophisticated modern version, has kept its traditional place under Zurich's Christmas trees up to this day.

Turkey

There is a Saint Nicholas and he lived in Turkey. So concludes Rex Miller after investigating, while on a foreign news assignment, the mass of myth and fiction that has gathered around the name and has transformed the generous bishop into our jolly Santa Claus so familiar to all of us. Only an almost forgotten group of ruins remain in the remote corner of southwestern Turkey where the true Saint Nicholas was born and became a bishop.

The Christian Turks observe a three-day festival filled with much visiting and entertaining in which coffee plays a prominent part along with sweetmeats, fruit, and sometimes, sour milk, a favorite among them.

Ukrainia

The Ukrainian Christmas falls on January 6, according to the Julian calendar. When the thirty-nine days' fast begins, people think of preparations for the Feast of the Nativity. On Christmas Eve the house is spick-and-span, a hearty fire is crackling in the oven, and the housewife is busy preparing a sumptuous twelve-course dinner, one course in memory of each of the twelve apostles. All of them must be prepared without meat, fish of some sort taking the place of meat. There will be *borsch* (a beet soup), cabbage, in the old country stuffed with millet but here with rice, and cooked dried fruit. For dessert there will be *kutya*, the exclusive Christmas Eve delicacy prepared from whole-wheat grains soaked for many hours and then seasoned with honey mixed with crushed poppy seeds.

Young and old wait for the signal that begins Christmas — the appearance of the first star in the sky. When the children shout: " The star! Mother, I see the star! " the time has come to begin the supper. The people speak for the most part in low tones. If there is peace and order, love and affection, on this eve, then it will prevail in this household till the Christmas that follows. When the supper is over, the children receive gifts of nuts and apples.

At midnight the family attends mass. Among Ukrainians in Europe, Christmas extends for three days. Singers known as *Kolyadniky* go from house to house singing folk songs that tell of the birth of Christ and the events of his life. They are rewarded by gifts of food and money.

These processions have been interestingly " Americanized." In the United States during Christmas week, representative men visit the Ukrainian households and collect money for the support of the educational enterprises undertaken by the Ukrainians in the old country. Generally they preface these requests with a few bars of song.

Yugoslavia (also Jugoslavia)

Each of the three principal racial groups constituting the Kingdom of the Serbs, Croats, and Slovenes had customs of its own before the union in 1918; the Serbians, who belong to the Greek Orthodox Church, from their co-religionists in the East, and the Slovenes and Croatians, from their German and Italian neighbors.

The Croats and Serbians both plant wheat on a plate on December 10. By Christmas Day there is a miniature field of wheat which serves as decoration. It is usually set on the window sill. They also have a yule log custom which is not found among the Slovenians. Before sunrise on Christmas morning, the men of the family go into a nearby forest to fell a young tree. They bring it back in state, and lighted candles are held on each side of the door through which it is carried into the home. Corn and wine are sprinkled on it, and sometimes it is wreathed with garlands. As soon as it is burning brightly, a neighbor, chosen beforehand for the ceremony, strikes the log sharply with a rod of iron or wood, and as the sparks fly from it, he chants his wishes for the prosperity of the family — that they may have as many horses and as many cattle as the sparks; that their harvest may be as bountiful; and other wishes of similar sort.

The Serbian strews his table with hay or straw at Christmas time, a reminder of the manger. At the Christmas Day dinner he, and also his Croatian brother, is likely to eat roasted suckling pig, which must be carved according to definite rites.

A dish peculiar to the Croatian Christmas is the *Kolach*, a ring-shaped coffeecake. Three candles are placed within its hollow. The first is lighted on Christmas Eve. The father of the family makes the sign of the cross with it, saying, " Christ is born," the other responding, " He is born indeed." The second candle is lighted at noon on Christmas Day; after a prayer it is blown out. The third is not lighted until New Year's Day, and the cake is not cut until the Three Kings' Day, January 6, when each member of the family gets a slice to symbolize his share in the good fortune of the coming year.

Every Slovenian household must have a Christmas crib, and it is also found in many Croatian homes. Expeditions to the forests to gather moss with which to line the crib are a Christmas custom widely observed. The cribs are usually elaborate. There is background representing Bethlehem, and images of the Christchild, the Virgin Mary, and Joseph, and sometimes also of the shepherds, the Three Kings, and the animals. Quite frequently there will be an old-fashioned music box that plays Christmas carols.

3. Christmas in the United States and Canada

CHRISTMAS in the United States is familiar to us all — the tree, caroling, the Christmas Eve midnight or Christmas morning church services, dinner with a turkey or a goose, pumpkin or mince pie, and all the trimmings. So it is needless to elaborate on these. It will be of more interest to note the great diversity in the forms of observing the season in the various sections of our land and in countries more or less closely related to us.

Before turning to these more serious matters, we can enter into one detail of the peculiarly American Christmas observance by noting the following poem:

FOR THE CHILDREN OR THE GROWNUPS?

'Tis the week before Christmas and every night
　As soon as the children are snuggled up tight
And have sleepily murmured their wishes and prayers,
　Such fun as goes on in the parlor downstairs!
For Father, Big Brother, and Grandfather too,
　Start in with great vigor their youth to renew.
The grownups are having great fun — all is well;
　And they play till it's long past their hour for bed.

They try to solve puzzles and each one enjoys
The magical thrill of mechanical toys.
Even Mother must play with a doll that can talk,
And if you assist it, it's able to walk.
It's really no matter if paint may be scratched,
Or a cogwheel, a nut, or a bolt gets detached;
The grownups are having great fun — all is well;
The children don't know it, and Santa won't tell.

THE UNITED STATES

Columbus on Haiti in December, 1492

Christopher Columbus entered the port of Bohio, on the island of Haiti, on Saint Nicholas Day, December 6, 1492, and named the port Saint Nicholas. When the *Santa María* was wrecked on a sandbank, the chief of the island sent a fleet of canoes to assist the strangers, and he also provided a feast of shrimps and bread for the several hundred men of Columbus' crew in addition to the several hundred natives who were present.

After these simple festivities, the work of building a fortress began at once. It was needed both as a home for those who could not find room in the *Niña* for the return trip and as a protection against the natives and wild animals. Providing a year's supply of biscuits, wine, and other provisions, Columbus bade farewell to the forty men he had to leave behind and sailed for Europe on January 4, 1493. According to the records related to the above, Columbus was the first European who received gifts during the Christmas season in America.

Jamestown, 1607 — from Solemnity to Cheer

Almost one hundred fifty years later Jamestown, Virginia, was settled, in 1607. Sailing December 19, 1606, the settlers spent their first Christmas within sight of their old homes. Captain John Smith reports that though many were ill, they " made the best cheer they could." The first yuletide in the new world was spent by Captain Smith as a captive of Powhatan, an Indian chief. With no women in the colony until 1609, when only twenty came, it is not surprising that no significant Christmas observance took place before 1619 when ninety more appeared.

Much as to the early difficulties is reflected in Captain Smith's journal: " The extreme winds, rayne, frost and snow caused us to keep Christmas among the savages, where we weere never more merry, nor fed on more plenty of good Oysters, Fish, Flesh, Wild Fowl and good bread, nor never had better fires in England."

When prosperity gradually came to the Jamestown colony, the settlers of Virginia became known for their hospitality with carriage loads of guests in old-time mansions enjoying weeks of good cheer and fun. For masters and slaves, in the " great house " and in cabins, it was a season of peace, plenty, and merriment. Churches were decorated with boughs of green and flowers, and church services struck the joyful note of the season.

Plymouth, 1620 — a Somber Christmas

The Puritans showed their disdain for this pagan festival by planning hard work for the day and passing a law forbidding the celebration of Christmas. Somewhat less somber was the attitude of the Pilgrims, who had absorbed something of the spirit of the day while living in Holland the previous years. The *Mayflower* brought a barrel full of ivy, holly, and laurel with which the tables were decorated and wreaths were woven for the children.

Early in the settlement and increasingly so for several decades, the Puritan spirit prevailed, but by May, 1659, the General Court of Massachusetts felt it necessary to enact a law establishing a fine of five shillings for those observing Christmas Day. Not until December 8, 1686, was a Christmas service conducted in Boston under legal sanction. In 1753, the Old South congregation offered its sanctuary to the worshipers in King's Chapel after that edifice was burned, but stipulated cautiously that no spruce, holly, or other greens should desecrate the meeting house.

Step by step the atmosphere changed in New England, and in 1856 the day was made a legal holiday in Massachusetts.

The Dutch Christmas of Good Cheer on Manhattan

Quite different was the situation among the Dutch. Christmas was a joyful season for them, with churches and quaint gabled houses trimmed with evergreens. The City Fathers " adjourned " from December 14 until three weeks after Christmas. On December 14, 1654, they ordered: " As the winter and the holidays are at hand, there shall be no more ordinary meetings of this board (the City Corporation) between this date and three weeks after Christmas. The Court Message is ordered not to summon anyone in the meantime."

Quite in harmony with such a resolution was the abundant preparation for Christmas, reflected so vividly in " A Visit from St. Nicholas." Trees, gifts, feasting with turkeys, pies and puddings, religious services — these were a prominent part of the Dutch Christmas spirit that these sturdy settlers had brought to our shores.

Among the Moravians

Weeks before Christmas the Moravian housewives in Bethlehem, Pennsylvania, and in other Moravian settlements are busy in their kitchens preparing *Kuemmelbrod*, sugar cake, mince pies, and large quantities of Christmas cookies cut in the shapes of animals, stars, Christmas trees, and little men and women. The Putz, a miniature landscape of moss, greens, and make-believe rocks, adorned with toy houses, tiny fences, trees, animals, and generally the Holy Family, is seldom missing under the tree.

On Christmas Eve the family attends the love feast at the church. While the choir is singing, a good-sized bun and a large cup of coffee is served to all as a token of fellowship. Before the end of the service, lighted wax candles on large trays are brought into the church and a candle is passed to each person to remind him of the coming of Him who is the Light of the World.

The Pennsylvania Germans

In addition to having adopted many of the Moravian Christmas customs just described, the Pennsylvania Germans give a prominent place to Pelznickel. " Look out, or Pelznickel will catch you," is the pre-Christmas warning held over naughty boys and girls. Though related to Santa Claus, he is not quite the same. Pelznickel means " fur Nicholas," since he is dressed in old clothes, with fur trimming and a white beard. Armed with a switch and a bag of toys, he rewards the good children and playfully taps the others with his switch.

Christmas in the Old South

Christmas on the plantation was not just a day for children — it was a season to be enjoyed by everyone, and the preparations began right after Thanksgiving with the baking and storing away of the first Christmas cakes. From then on it was one grand and glorious round of " fixin'."

The land itself provided all but a few of the " store-bought'n " gifts — the pigs for roasting, the hams, the turkeys, and all the delicious puddings and dressings, preserves, jellies, jams, pickles, peppers, sweet potatoes, nuts, and all the countless delights of Southern cooking. The woods and fields provided the hickory logs and pine knots for the fireplace; the holly, mistletoe, and evergreen boughs, for the decorations; the partridges and rabbits, to round out the Christmas menus.

Everything was cleaned and polished to shining perfection, and when Christmas Eve arrived the plantation was rich with color and sound. When the old cowbell rang summoning everyone to the watch-night meeting in the Quarters, Christmas Eve had arrived. Solemn old hymns were sung until midnight, and prayers were offered by the earnest voices. With the arrival of cock's-crow announcing the holy hour, the prayers turned to rejoicing and dancing and singing — and it was Christmas! Then everyone rushed into the Big House with a shouted " Christmas Gift," and with games, feasting, and song, the week-long festival was launched. It was again Christmas in the old South.

Many persons continue the shooting of firearms and firecrackers in this season — not only in our South but in Hawaii and in the Philippines. To the girls and boys of the South, Christmas is noisier and jollier than the Fourth of July by far. Some believe the custom originated in the days when the early settlers sent Christmas greetings by this means to distant neighbors. Others suggest that the practice goes back to the idea of making noises to frighten away evil spirits.

" Going Round with the Star " in Alaska

This land has one half the area of the entire United States, and a coast line longer than the country it has joined as the forty-ninth state. While the Christmas observances among the Christians who have migrated there are similar to those of the countries from which they came, the natives have for years been " going round with the star." A large figure of a star, covered with brightly colored paper, is taken from door to door by boys and girls carrying lanterns on long poles. After singing carols, they are welcomed inside for refreshments.

This continues through Christmas week, but after the second night the star-bearers are followed by another party of boys and girls, sometimes by adults too, dressed to represent Herod's soldiers, trying to capture the star and to destroy it as Herod's men tried to destroy the infant Jesus.

A Summer Christmas in Hawaii

Christmas was unknown in Hawaii before the missionaries and the American settlements came. While it is now celebrated much as in the United States, the weather is like our June. Vegetation is profuse; sunny skies smile on gardens. In the morning religious services are attended, and during the rest of the day there are games and merrymaking. The Christmas dinner is eaten outdoors.

The natives claim Santa Claus comes to the islands in a boat. That sounds quite natural. At any rate he gets there, and the children look forward to his coming as do their cousins in the United States.

The Pastores in the Philippines

Christmas is a great religious festival for the Filipino. On Christmas Eve the churches are open, and the coming of the birthday of the Lord is celebrated by a mass at midnight. The day is ushered in early in the morning by the ringing of bells for hours. During all of Christmas Day, mass is held every hour to give everyone an opportunity to attend. Most of the popular Christmas customs partake of a religious character, little plays as dramas picturing the Nativity forming a large part.

These plays, called *pastores*, are performed by young men and young women who go from village to village portraying, in simple, crude fashion, the incidents related in Scripture.

After the church services, there is a floral procession of the children, singing carols and parading through the streets led by a band.

Everybody, from the beggars on the street corners to the policeman, comes to the door with a " Merry Christmas," in return expecting a greeting accompanied with something tangible, some coins. And this is repeated at New Year's! Similarly annoying, though in a slightly different way, is the shooting of firecrackers, starting in November and continuing practically every night through the festive season.

A more enjoyable and appealing part of the season is the lantern contest. Boys and girls make paper lanterns of different shapes and colors. Candles are placed inside, and at night the parade down the street is a beautiful sight to behold.

The American Indians

While the vast majority of the American Indians still follow their ancient superstitions, appeasing the evil spirits under the direction of their medicine men, a small minority are being ministered to regularly by Christian missionaries. It is estimated that two thirds of them cannot speak or understand the English language. To see the Christian leaven at work, especially in the Christmas season, we turn to two tribes — the Navahos and the Pimas.

The *Navahos* are the largest tribe in the United States, numbering over 80,000 and growing at the rate of more than 1,000 per year. They do not live in villages but are widely scattered, moving about in seminomadic fashion, with their flocks and herds, across the rough desert country. The United States Government has set aside a 25,000 square-mile territory in Arizona, New Mexico, and a part of southern Utah. Their homes are called hogans and are made of logs and mud plaster.

Thanks to devoted Christian missionaries, Christmas does find its way to these people. It is one significant demonstration of their love for them. The news the " Kismus " time is at hand travels from hogan to hogan. This includes a " big feed " at the Shonto Trading Post. By ten o'clock on Christmas Day, a thousand people have gathered awaiting the sumptuous meal and gifts, generally a special treat provided by an interested friend. The meal consists of meat, beans, potatoes, and onions, boiled in two huge iron pots hung over a campfire. Several tubs of coffee, innumerable doughnuts and cases of bread and buns, complete the menu. By eleven o'clock the lines form — women and children first, then the elderly men, finally the young men. Having their old plates, tin cans, or other receptacles filled, they gather with friends at one of the many campfires provided.

After dinner, stacks of clothing, towels, wash cloths, and toys are provided, as well as fruits and candies. When the sun begins to set over the red rock canyon walls of Shonto, the people slip away as quietly as they have come, appreciative of the unselfish devoted love demonstrated to them on " Kismus " Day.

More distinctly Christian is the observance of the season among the *Pimas* at Salt River Indiana Reservation, near Phoenix, Arizona. On Christmas Eve the choir is busy rehearsing at church, and women are busy preparing chickens for the morrow.

When the clock strikes twelve, all make their way homeward — some in cars, some in wagons, and the rest on foot. Early the next morning strains of " Silent Night! Holy Night! " are heard coming from under the big pepper tree at the church. Then follows " Joy to the World," and soon the families arrive, mothers carrying babies on one arm and kettles on the other.

After a bounteous meal, a siesta under the trees is in order. Later the babies continue to sleep, the children play, and the grownups visit together. At dusk all gather in the church for the program — songs, recitations, even the " Hallelujah Chorus." After the program Santa brings toys and sweets. When all have been remembered, they start for home. Another joyful Christmas Day has come and gone.

CANADA

Like the United States, Canada observes the festive season in diversified forms in its various provinces. So we shall presently survey these briefly but first take note of:

An Eskimo Christmas

The children of the Far North know of the Christmas story only what the white man has told them. But before the white man visited them, the Eskimos had a big midwinter festival, *Sinck tuck*, a big dance and present-giving party.

It is unique in that it is an event between towns or villages. One invites the other, and the next winter the entertained village returns the compliment. The heart of it consists of folk dances in costumes of fur, trimmed with feathers and ornaments of ivy; feasting on rare delicacies; and the grand finale, present-giving.

On the appointed day, a long, picturesque caravan of dog teams arrives, bringing every member of the village, even the ill and the crippled, who may need assistance. The dancing lasts for days, as long as the entertaining village can produce feasting, provisions, and entertainment. So it is a season of good will and merriment for all.

How such a spirit, and form as well, can be changed is indicated in the paragraphs below, as we turn to:

Labrador

Grenfell's work among the fisherfolk of Labrador has led them into an entirely new type of life, part of the motivating change being due to the observance of Christmas in the mission churches founded by him on this peninsula.

The children enjoy receiving little lighted candles standing in a turnip that has been specially saved from the harvest for this use. In earlier years the candles were made of deer tallow and hence were edible along with the turnip, but more recently the imported candles compel the children to miss this part of the treat.

Newfoundland

During Christmas week it is customary for the folks to " fish for the church." They bring their catch to be sold for the local parish. Quite frequently contributions also make possible a big load of wood for the curate.

Nova Scotia (New Scotland)

In the part of the Cape Breton country settled by Scottish highlanders, the psalms resound on Christmas morning. And in other sections, people, either in their white-walled cottages or in their houses of worship, sing old songs and carols which their ancestors brought from the Basque country and from Britanny two centuries ago.

Vancouver

Gaily illuminated Christmas trees glow softly in the homes, on the lawns, and in the squares of this Western city. In its harbor with eighty miles of water frontage, red and green lights show where ships are waiting to go to Great Britain, Australia, China, Japan, and other countries, laden with fir and cedar from the forests, with salmon from the sea, and with grain from the prairies. In this picturesque city, too, the Christmas spirit takes a form largely parallel with the other cities of the Dominion.

So throughout its vast expanse, Canada celebrates the festive season religiously and joyfully.

4. Christmas in Central America and the West Indies

TO MOST readers Christmas comes in the winter, with snow or thoughts of snow; but Latin America greets Christmas with weather like our midsummer. December there is the season of bright flowers and ripe fruits. Therefore Christmas can take on only as much of the color and forms of observances " as the weather permits," and even then adapt them considerably to the different circumstances. Since the definitely religious observances are relatively untouched by this factor, the matter is, of course, not serious. For example, the manger, which is so central a part, conveys its message regardless of the temperature. In churches and in homes the *Nacimiento* (Spanish for " manger ") receives central attention.

It is to be noted, however, that through modern communication and travel, gradually Santa Claus is appearing even in the larger cities of Latin America, a few Christmas trees are imported, and the exchange of gifts is being accepted more and more.

On Christmas Eve people stroll along the streets where vendors offer fruits and refreshment. The music of guitars, castanets, and gourds fills the air. Suddenly when the church bell calls, the streets are deserted, since all go to midnight mass. Some attend again on Christmas morning. Either on Christmas Eve or on Christmas Day, families gather for roast suckling pig, hot foamy chocolate, and cakes. The afternoon is passed with picnics, bull fights, and other diversions. Sometimes a procession is formed, led by two people carrying a manger, followed by gaily costumed children singing Christmas songs.

The day for exchanging gifts is not Christmas but January 6 (Twelfth-night), when traditionally the Wise Men brought their gifts to Jesus. The children put their shoes in the window to be filled with toys and candies.

Costa Rica

In this island country there is a variation of the *presepio* known as the *portal*. Instead of a manger scene under the tree or in a corner of a room, a whole room is filled with a replica of the Nativity, and people go from house to house admiring them.

The Christ-child has for centuries been accepted as the giver of gifts, but recently Santa Claus has also made his influence felt here. It is not uncommon to see a manikin in a department-store window, equipped with a beard and the rest of the Santa-Claus regalia.

The Dominican Republic

Christmas here remains a religious holiday. The Christmas dinner is enjoyed generally after the Christmas Eve midnight mass. Carols are sung in the streets.

Through trade and social relations with the United States, Santa Claus is becoming increasingly popular, but the children continue to receive their presents on January 6, when gold, frankincense, and myrrh were traditionally given by the Wise Men.

Honduras

The Christmas celebration in Honduras, largely Roman Catholic, is preceded by nine days of seeking lodging for the holy pilgrims, Joseph and Mary. A house in the town is designated to which the faithful go each night of the nine, chanting hymns on the streets and before the house, interspersed by prayers. The family offering the house for the purpose receives a special blessing from the priest. Masses are held in the churches during the holidays and Bethlehem scenes, *Nacimientos*, are reproduced in the homes. The Sunday schools have their programs at night. Both then and afterward on the street, carol-singing is winning in favor. It is frequently carried on in the native Spanish, in English for the North Americans, and in German for a large group of immigrants. Since many of the poorer people do not have trees or toys for the children, the missions are especially popular in the festive season. People come from hill farms and banana camps to admire the trees and toys, and thus come under the influence of the spirit of God's love of which all these external things are but an expression.

Special food is prepared, of which tamales are very popular. They are made of corn meal, meat (generally pork), and peas. The corn meal covers the meat and vegetables, and the entire tamale is wrapped in a banana leaf and cooked (generally steamed) in a kettle. They are served with a little pepper, less hot than in Mexico.

Dances, fireworks, visits in the homes of friends and especially to the *Nacimientos* fill the holidays for the masses.

Mexico, the Land of Posadas

While general preparations for Christmas extend to several weeks before Christmas in the United States, in Mexico the home must be decorated and ready to receive guests, not by December 24, but by December 16, the beginning of the Mexican *posadas*. The word means resting place, lodging, or inn and is applied to the Mexican custom of commemorating the trials and hardships experienced by Mary and Joseph in their attempt to find shelter in Bethlehem. After the house has been decorated with festoons of Spanish moss, evergreen branches, and colored paper lanterns, a little altar covered with pine branches and moss is erected in one room. On this altar is a representation of the Nativity, the shepherds with their flocks, small huts, and trees. In the center there is a small hill on whose summit is a stable containing the figures of Mary and Joseph contemplating an empty cradle.

Families go to one another's homes, and as the guests arrive they are divided into two groups — the cruelhearted innkeepers and the holy pilgrims. Each one of the pilgrims is provided with a candle. The procession marches through the corridors of the house.

The pilgrims begin to sing, asking shelter, and a dialogue in song ensues between the pilgrims and the innkeepers, more or less in this manner:

" Who knocks at my door, so late in the night? "
" We are pilgrims, without shelter, and we want only a place
    to rest."
" Go somewhere else and disturb me not again."
" But the night is very cold. We have come from afar, and we
    are very tired."
" But who are you? I know you not."
" I am Joseph of Nazareth, a carpenter, and with me is Mary,
    my wife, who will be the mother of the Son of God."
" Then come into my humble home, and welcome! And may
    the Lord give shelter to my soul when I leave this world! "

Then the doors of the living room are opened, and the procession enters with joyous songs, proceeding then to say prayers, different each night, but similar to the following:

O God, who, in coming to save us, didst not disdain a humble stable, grant that we may never close our hearts when thou art knocking so that we may be made worthy to be received into thy sight when our hour comes.

With these prayers the strictly religious part of the *posadas* comes to an end. There follows, especially among the children, a period of frivolity. The group gathers in the patio for a display of fireworks and the enjoyment of candies and fruits, but most especially for the *piñata*.

The *piñata*, which is suspended in the center of the patio, is an earthenware jar, gaily decorated with gold and silver paper and colored-tissue fringe and streamers. The jar is made in a great variety of sizes and shapes, and one may suit one's fancy with anything from a small plain round one to such fantastic ones as flying birds, airplanes, dolls, or fairies. The children come one by one, blindfolded, and provided with a stick, to try to break the *piñata*, which has been liberally filled with fruits, nuts, and sweetmeats. Finally, some lucky child breaks it with his stick, and its contents are spilled onto the floor, whereupon the happy youngsters scramble to get as much of the fruit and candies as possible.

The last of the *posadas*, on Christmas Eve, is the most solemn and impressive of all. At the end of the prayer, to the singing of special songs, a small image of the infant Jesus is placed in the cradle. The candles are lighted around the altar, and all join in: " Alleluia! Alleluia! Let us rejoice because the Lord has come to his people! Let us sing praises to the Lord. Come ye, sing and rejoice! Blessed is he that cometh in the name of the Lord. Hosanna in the highest! "

After the usual festivities of each of the nine evenings preceding, the entire family goes on Christmas Eve to the celebration of midnight mass. Christmas Day is passed more or less quietly at home. Santa Claus and Christmas trees are rare. The children receive their toys and gifts on Epiphany, January 6, having put their shoes in the window the night before.

The Protestant *posadas* are considerably modified. The visitors congregate with lighted candles outside the house and sing a hymn suggesting Christ knocking at the door of our hearts and seeking lodging. The persons inside answer in song, the door is opened, and a crowd enters, varying from twenty to one hundred persons. Some sit on chairs, but most of the children sit on grass mats on the floor, and all enjoy singing Christmas carols for some twenty minutes. Then a child stands and recites or reads Luke 2:1-7. All sing a hymn, and another child quotes Luke 1:8-20. Then someone gives a talk on the meaning of Christmas — why our Lord came to this earth. After an hour of song and worship, there is an hour of games and fun, perhaps including a *piñata* as described above, and the visit ends with refreshments.

Characteristic of Protestant Christmas observances is also the Christmas Eve program. It usually begins around eight or eight thirty. About nine o'clock the church is full, and people are standing in the street, looking and listening to Christmas poems, songs, and plays. The program lasts until eleven o'clock. Then comes the most exciting time for the children who go to Sabbath school. Even if they are asleep, they are awakened to receive their gift and bag from Santa Claus. When all the gifts have been distributed, it is about twelve o'clock. So everyone is ready to go home.

On Christmas night and the following five nights, programs are held out in the ranches. The boys and girls from the ranches present some numbers, and then a group from Rio Verde presents numbers. As very few, if any, of the people in the ranch ever see a picture show, they are thrilled to learn of the birth and life of Christ as shown and told in pictures. This is one time most of the people who live in the ranch attend services. After the picture, the children who attend Sabbath school have their " tree."

Nicaragua

Nicaragua, like most Latin American countries, retains many customs of Old Spain. Christmas here may be called the Festival of Childhood. Before the end of November, children begin to throng the streets, carrying fragrant bouquets for the altar of the Virgin and singing carols to the Queen of Heaven. This pre-Christmas celebration reaches its peak on December 8, the Feast of the Immaculate Conception. Not until midnight does the sound of horns, of the marimbas, and even of the merry-makers themselves, fade away.

On December 16, the faithful begin their annual novena to the Holy Child, and on December 24 it is concluded with the midnight mass.

By December 24, the palm trees, green sawdust, tinsel, and colored lights decorate the home, centering around the empty manger, which receives the figure of the infant Jesus at midnight. Toys, sweets, and other gifts are distributed, and a Christmas Eve feast is common. This will consist, according to the purse of the family, of turkey, a stuffed hen, or the humbler tamales. The tamale is made of ground corn, with a filling of turkey, chicken, or pork, and raisins, almonds, olives, and chili, wrapped in banana leaves. Wine, coffee, or chocolate may be served with plain cake for dessert, made with corn meal or rice flour and covered with rum-flavored sirup.

Lately, the Christmas tree — usually artificial — laden with colored balls, wreaths, and icicles, with gifts beneath it, has been introduced.

Panama

While Christmas remains a religious festival in Panama, it is also a holiday for children and young people; and it is the occasion for intimate family gatherings for adults. For the nine days preceding Christmas, carols are sung at the special masses held at dawn, and are very popular with the young people.

In the early hours of Christmas Eve children and grownups visit the *Nacimientos* (manger scenes) in churches and in private homes. The guests are served wines, nuts, raisins, and a variety of nougats and traditional Christmas sweets.

Children participate in the midnight mass by singing Spanish carols, accompanied by castanets and tambourines. Among the most popular are " Lullaby of the Christ Child," " Come, Little Shepherds," and " Silent Night! Holy Night! " (For Spanish words of the last mentioned, see *Carols, Customs and Costumes Around the World.*)

After the church services, the families return home for the Christmas meal. Among the dishes are turkey stuffed with chopped fresh pork, hard-boiled eggs, onions, olives, raisins, and other garnishes.

The *Nacimientos* are often very elaborate and artistic, and the figures and decorations are kept from year to year for their preparation. Not only the manger scene itself, but miniature houses, trees, plants, waterfalls, grass, etc., represent the town of Bethlehem and surrounding country, with animals, shepherds, and the Holy Kings bringing gifts, to illustrate the Christmas story.

At school several classroom projects lead up to the one-day holiday on Christmas Day. Besides preparing the *Nacimiento* for the schoolroom, children learn carols, make and exchange *aguinaldos* (Christmas gifts) and handmade greeting cards, prepare plays and pageants, and write letters, promising their very best behavior, to the Baby Jesus, in Heaven, % Saint Peter, and closing the letters by sending kisses and greetings to Joseph and the Virgin Mary.

The Christmas season is very beautiful and joyous; it is the end of the rainy season, and nature is green and radiant; breezes are cool; red poinsettias are in full bloom, under the mild tropical sun. In the villages, the adobe houses have been newly whitewashed. It is the time for picking the red coffee beans, the cashews, and oranges, mangoes, and other tropical fruits; the time for cutting sugar cane and for preparing homemade preserves and sweets, such as candied cashew nuts, preserves of green papayas, cashews, fruits, mangoes, and sun-dried, figlike bananas. Children, looking forward to the long school vacation (February to April), are busy making and flying kites and playing other seasonal games.

Puerto Rico

While Christmas trees are being shipped from New England to Puerto Rico and Santa Claus is being welcomed increasingly, Christmas continues to have a distinctly religious tone.

The major part of the more festive aspect centers around January 6, Three Kings' Day, as it is known there. The Three Kings go from house to house, dressed in elaborate costumes. They bring presents, mostly fruits.

The children are taught to expect gifts, not from Santa Claus, but from the Three Kings. They gather grass at the river banks and place it under their beds or on the roofs as food for the camels, expecting, in return, the boxes to be filled with toys and gifts.

Open house is held for three days — January 6, 7, and 8 — when the men go from house to house playing their guitars. Early in the morning, callers begin to arrive and the hostess is expected to greet them with an impromptu song composed to apply to each individual visitor.

Another colorful celebration is known as "Bethlehem Day," January 12, when children, in memory of the Magi, form a procession through the streets led by three children. They are dressed as the Wise Men, ride on ponies or horses, and hold gifts for the infant King in their hands. Then follow numerous angels, shepherds, and flute players.

As in most other countries, considerable eating and drinking accompany the observance of the season.

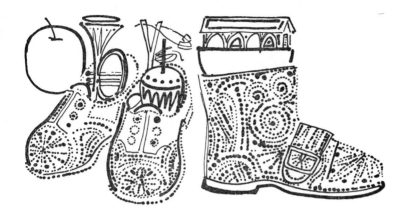

5. Christmas in South America

THE VARIED national backgrounds and the warmer weather of the Christmas season combine to encourage South America to retain many of its traditional customs and to allow North American and Anglo-Saxon ways to enter but slowly.

Common to most South American countries, along with Latin America, is the *presepio* (the manger) and the *Missa do Gallo* (the midnight Christmas Eve mass) followed by the singing of carols. Though the lines cannot always be sharply drawn, generally there are some detailed differences as to festive observances in each country. We shall refer to several typical ones here.

Argentina

Christmas dawns in midsummer, when hot and dry winds, called *zonda*, blow from the north. Either a Christmas Eve mass or an early Christmas morning mass commemorates the Nativity. The altar is specially decorated with the Nativity scenes, though the figures may be crude and disproportionate at times.

Christmas dinner is generally served outside under the shade of a tree, a trellis, or on a veranda. On the table, which is beautifully decorated with rose buds and jasmine, a roasted suckling pig is placed at the center. In addition, pieces of steak, three inches square, rolled and stuffed with mincemeat seasoned with olives, hard-boiled eggs, and spices, form part of the menu.

The day is observed comparatively quietly, the festivities being delayed until New Year's and in part until January 6, Three Kings' Day, when, on the latter, the children place their shoes by the side of the bed, hoping to have them filled with toys and gifts before morning. They never forget to set water and hay outside the door so that the horses (or camels) of the Magi will be strengthened for their long journey!

Brazil

Brazil is a vast country, and gradually, in addition to the Christmas observances brought over from Portugal, the season gathers about itself some features and traditions that reflect local backgrounds and circumstances. The very fact that the season falls in midsummer is a significant modifying factor, occasioning the varied and alluring characteristics of summertime festivals, such as fireworks, picnics, open-air " fiestas," boating excursions, and similar diversions.

Then, too, Christmas is doubly welcome to the young folks because it comes directly after the final examinations, school festivals, and closing exercises, and ushers in the longer school vacation with the prospects of home-coming, travel, rest, and relaxation.

While the mass and the manger are universal, there are also folk songs and folk dances. Open-air dancing and carols often occupy the time leading up to the Christmas preceding the midnight mass. Poetry contests involving verses accompanied by guitars are often featured on Three Kings' Day. In the homes of the prosperous, balls, banquets, and entertainments are frequent from December 24 to January 6.

Early in December, everyone in the Brazilian home hustles about setting up the crèche, with the Christ-child lying in the manger, and around him, Joseph, Mary, and the Magi. This representation of the Nativity may be very simple, but occasionally it becomes exceedingly elaborate, perhaps filling one or more rooms of the house. It is often a delightful hodgepodge of glaring anachronisms, in which the pastoral calm of Bethlehem mingles with the latest developments of the machine age: the shepherds out on the plain, overcome with the heavenly vision; wild grottoes; barren deserts; little white wells; Brazilian water mills; electric trains speeding on furiously, as though seized with a frenzy; white sailboats or up-to-date steamers plying the blue waters of the sea; and daring planes flying low over the picturesque stable; it forms a comprehensive interpretation of the past in which all human achievements are summoned and innocently and tenderly presented to the Holy Child.

In the larger Brazilian cities the more conservative families still keep the traditional Christmas. The whole family gather together. Through the open windows comes a playful breeze and the sound of music, dancing, and merry conversation. The children may enjoy their own amusements, possibly a game of forfeits or the singing of *rodas*, a game in which they join hands and go through various gestures as they sing traditional songs.

As midnight draws near, all find their way to church. When they return home, the tempting aroma of the Christmas supper welcomes them. There is usually the roast pig and not uncommonly a steamed fish pie made of corn meal, cassana flour, sardines, and shrimp — or it may be that fried shrimp is the center of the meal — in all cases followed by a bewildering assortment of Brazilian desserts.

Through foreign influence and intercourse, jolly old Santa Claus and most of the things we associate with him have been competing with established traditions. He is known there as *Papa Noël*. Toys are on display in the markets, and Christmas trees are taking their place alongside of *presepios*, substituting bits of cotton and glittery tinsel for snow. Years ago there was an attempt to replace Santa with a more native Grandpapa Indian, but Santa merely chuckled and continued to win his way, even though literally " in the sweat of his brow." The traditional chimney, however, had to be dropped, since hardly any houses are equipped with such things.

Here, as we have also seen in Latin America, Protestant missions have introduced the white-gift Christmas observance. While many of the people are poor, they generally know of others who are in still greater need. So each person brings a little gift of food, a bit of rice, a potato or two, if he can spare no more — anything to help make a Christmas dinner for some poorer person in the community. Children and adults come with enthusiasm and joy. All gifts are wrapped in white paper, and there, in the front of the church, around a crude little manger filled with straw and a small light, symbolic of the " Light of the World," they walk to the front with their gifts, singing as they go! They learn and express that not receiving but giving is the real spirit of Christmas.

" Trimming the Tree in Brazil " not only so vividly describes this part of the Christian observance but also reflects so splendidly the spirit that is gaining ground that we furnish it in detail for our readers. It is taken from the *Presbyterian Survey*, December, 1949.

It was Christmas Eve, and two eager, little faces were watching the clock. Neither could tell the time as yet, but big sister Norma had said that when the big hand reached twelve and the little hand was at eight, Daddy would be back from his last round of seeing the patients in the Goldsby King Hospital next door.

Daddy's coming meant that the family would then trim the tree. Hadn't big brother Wilson helped bring it in that morning? Antonio Eugenio, four years old, and Hildinha, two, could scarcely wait. Sister Thais, just eight, was almost as excited as they were, but she was talking fast about what " Papa Noël " (Santa Claus) might bring each of them, to make the time pass more quickly.

" Daddy is here, children! " called Dona Hilda. That was the signal from their lovely mother, and the magic word for which they were waiting. Everyone helped. Dr. Duarte and the older children draped strings of popcorn, tissue paper cut in fancy shapes, and metal bells in the hard-to-reach places, while mother aided the smaller ones with the ornaments on the lower branches. How pretty the sour orange tree from the woods looked as it took on its Christmas dress!

The air was balmy and the windows were open. The light of a full moon showed the beautiful flowers in a large garden just outside and the roses shed their fragrance. The world is a lovely place in Brazil at Christmas time, for December is a summer month. The neighbors enjoyed the strains of hymns that came through the open windows of the Duarte home. As the family trimmed the tree, Mother would start first one carol and then another, and all would join her. Then she told again the Christmas story in words that the little ones could understand. Then Daddy told the legend of the first Christmas tree. When he got to the place where the poor little pine tree was very, very lonely and sad, tiny Hildinha's face fell, until Antonio Eugenio quickly added with big bright eyes: " But right away the little tree was happy when all the stars in heaven fell down to make him pretty and shining! "

They talked of the less fortunate children and friends who did not have the blessings of parents and a home, or who were too poor to celebrate. Tomorrow they would take sweets or plates of food to these in the neighborhood and that would be more fun to which to look forward!

And now the tree was ready. They looked at it in admiration; and the little ones danced, clapped their hands, and squealed with delight. Tomorrow they would see another tree at the hospital and little trees beside each bed; and at the church for the Christmas program! How many lovely things ahead! Now that the ceremonies were over, the children brought their shoes to place under the tree. Tomorrow early they would find them full of presents. The older children and Mother and Daddy brought packages wrapped in holiday attire to put under the tree. Each had saved and made things, so that all would be remembered, and that included the servants.

Usually family prayers were right after dinner, but on Christmas Eve they followed the trimming of the tree. It was a special treat to stay up later, and the excitement of anticipation kept them wide awake. Grandmother and the servants joined the circle in the living room. Daddy opened the Bible at Luke, ch. 2, and all listened attentively as he read about the first Christmas. Antonio Eugenio insisted on reciting the Twenty-third Psalm, even if it *was* Christmas Eve, for he had only recently learned it, although he still needed help with the " *surely goodness and mercy* "! Mother accompanied the carolers on the piano, and they sang " Silent Night! Holy Night! " and then there were prayers of gratitude for the Christ-child who is the Savior of the world.

Chile

Aside from the customs that Chile observes in common with neighboring countries, it has two unique ones — a Christmas fiesta at Andacollo honoring the virgin, and a grand fiesta that features horse racing chiefly.

Near La Serena, in Chile, is the little town of Andacollo. Some thirty thousand visitors gather here to pay homage to the virgin. Legend claims that an Indian woodcutter named Collo had a vision in which a celestial figure spoke to him, " Go, Collo, to the hills where wealth and happiness await you." Obedient to the vision, he did so, and his hatchet struck a statue of the virgin, some three feet high. He placed it on an altar in his hut, and thereafter increasing numbers came to worship her there.

In the festive season numerous dancers perform, garbed in red, blue, and green costumes, and the statue of the virgin is displayed, surrounded by a carved wooden frame of massed roses. Her gold crown contains emeralds and precious stones. She is known as the Virgin del Rosario. On the streets are vendors selling dolls, trinkets, handkerchiefs, and hot-meat pies.

The other fiesta is less religious but it is to be considered merely as an expression of the festive spirit. It is much like our county fairs in form. Beautiful spirited race horses are the main attraction but booths display beautiful Indian workmanship in rugs, blankets, and hand-wrought jewelry.

Colombia

As the eve of Christmas settles down over the cities, towns, and villages of Colombia, a foreigner peeping into the houses, large and small, rich and poor, will look upon a scene no doubt already familiar to him. He will see Christmas trees, pine branches, Spanish moss, flowers, and, in a prominent place in the living room, the *pesebre* (Christmas crib). The cribs may be simple or elaborate, according to the means of the family, but all will surely have their background of fine blue muslin strewn with silver stars; their small clay figures, some of them imported from far-off countries, and others, perhaps the majority, made by native craftsmen in Ráquira and other Colombian villages; the Holy Family, the shepherds with their sheep, and the Three Kings, and houses, barns, and lakes; and giving light and life to the whole, there will be glimmering candles and small colored lanterns. The central part of it all is the Christ-child, or *Niño Dios*. Gathered round the crib will be the children, singing *villancicos*, old Christmas carols, to the accompaniment of guitars and other stringed instruments.

But if the stranger stays a little longer, he will witness a Christmas Eve custom that will undoubtedly be different from those he may have observed elsewhere. He may even for a moment lose his sense of time and think that it is Halloween or Mardi Gras, for at about nine o'clock on Christmas Eve, in Bogotá, in Popayán, in small towns in the Departments of Cauca and Tolima, and in many other places, he will see happy laughing groups of people coming out of the houses, dressed in masquerade costumes. For Christmas Eve is the night of the *aguinaldos*, or presents, when everyone disguises himself with fancy dress and mask and goes out to make merry in the streets. But the merrymaking and masquerade have a definite plan too. The idea is that everyone tries to recognize a friend in spite of the disguise, and when someone's identity is discovered, the discerning person claims an *aguinaldo*, or gift, from the one he recognized. This jolly custom is especially popular with the young people, and above all with sweethearts, for the disguises are kept secret and each tries to outwit the other and be the first to win the *aguinaldo*.

As midnight approaches, it will be observed that the masqueraders disappear from the streets, and a stillness descends that is broken at last by the glad peal of the church bells, calling the populace to the midnight mass. After the mass, which everyone attends, families and friends gather in their homes for the customary Christmas Eve repast. This is a rich feast of tamales, chicken or turkey, or roast pig, and for dessert, of course, *bunuelos* (see Chapter 9, Colombia) served with golden honey.

The feasting and fun continue among the grownups until the early morning hours, but the children, wiser than their elders and full of confidence, go off to bed, first carefully placing their shoes on the window sills or in the corridors. They know that while they sleep, the Christ-child and the Three Kings will come to fill the shoes with a long-anticipated store of toys and bonbons. The Holy Son, not Santa Claus, brings gifts to the children in Colombia.

Peru

In Lima, the capital, Christmas is a church holiday. However, not so exclusively as to crowd out the year's greatest bull fight! Following that feature of the holiday season, an elaborate procession is formed, at the head of which a statue of the virgin is carried. That ends the organized activities of the day; then the people enjoy themselves as they desire.

In the Christmas season the markets are crowded. The Indian merchants have toys, trinkets, and delicacies spread out on mats on the ground. By Christmas Eve the crowds are a jostling multitude, laughing and singing to the music of castanets and guitars. Indians are making their way through the crowds with ice pails on their heads, calling, " Helado! Helado! " and the ice stalls are crowded with perspiring pleasure-seekers, for the night is generally hot and sultry. Great masses of greenery have been brought down from the mountains. The mangers have been provided for churches and homes. Indians travel many miles to make these shrines for their patrons.

Lima, the " City of One Hundred Churches," holds particularly beautiful and impressive processions.

When the midnight bell strikes, all is quiet. The people drop on their knees in prayer, and when they rise at the last stroke, they wish each other a *Noche Buena* (a good, or holy, night). Some of the oldest Spanish Christmas carols were sung in Lima as early as the sixteenth century. Most of them are sung after the midnight mass and are gay and vivacious with tambourine and castanet accompaniment. As in the United States, carolers go from house to house, receiving, after their songs, refreshments, and gifts known as *aguinaldo*.

Venezuela

For Venezuelans, as for the nationals of other Christian countries, Christmas means a mixture of religious commemoration and pagan entertainment. It means *Misa del Aguinaldo* (early morning mass) from December 16 to 24; the *Nacimiento* (crib) or *Pesebre* (manger); and *hallacas*, the never-failing Christmas dish.

The main celebration takes place on *Noche Buena* (Christmas Eve) and is one of the occasions of the year when all the children get together at their parents' home, to partake, after going to *Misa del Gallo* (midnight mass), of *hallacas* prepared by the mother and *dulce de lechoza*, the indispensable dessert made of green papaya and brown sugar. *Hallaca* is made of corn meal, with pork and chicken stuffing and numerous other delicacies, and wrapped in plantain leaves to make a sort of pie.

Practically no home fails to display a *Nacimiento*, set up December 16 and kept until January 6, the Day of the Three Wise Men. The little statues of the infant Jesus, the virgin mother, the ox and the donkey, the shepherds and Wise Men, become relics tenderly kept in the family for generations and replaced only when they are beyond mending.

A more ambitious *Nacimiento* is the *pesebre*. This represents an entire region with mountains, hills, plains, and valleys. The central point is the replica of the manger at Bethlehem. The structure is a framework covered with canvas and painted accordingly. Often this is a work of art into which the head of the family puts all his ingenuity, to the point of scaling all the figures and reproducing the country of Galilee as his imagination dictates. Sometimes it is a hodgepodge of figures of all sizes and periods.

The *pesebre* is placed in the living room and is open to the public during these three weeks of the Christmas season. In the evening, pilgrimages of boys and girls, as well as of older people, make the rounds of the *pesebres*.

The exchange of gifts, as practiced in the United States, is not customary in Venezuela. Children used to get their presents only on January 6, the Day of the Three Wise Men. Now, to their delight, the custom of giving them presents *also* on Christmas Day is being introduced! Saint Nick, at times, leaves presents on the children's beds. There is no snow for Santa's sled and no chimney for him to climb down. But in this country, as in others noted above, artificial trees serve frequently. And in any case, cotton, as artificial snow, delights the hearts of all.

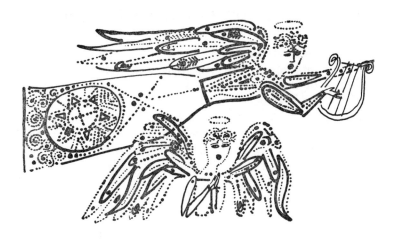

6. Christmas in Africa

IN AFRICA, as we shall see in Australia, we must remember three groups of people if we are to secure a fairly clear picture as to the observance of Christmas on the vast, promising continent. First, there are the native Negroes, the great majority untouched by Christianity and therefore unaware of the significance of the season that has come to mean so much to hundreds of millions of people.

Secondly, there are the Christian groups, who have in some cases had a continuous history there from the first century onward (Egypt, Ethiopia — the Coptic Church) and who in other cases have immigrated from Europe, especially into the area that developed into the Union of South Africa (the Anglican Church, the Reformed Church of Holland, and various smaller groups).

Finally, there are the younger churches which are the result of the modern missionary work of European and American boards and agencies.

Naturally, the customs of the last two groups reflect their own backgrounds and must be interpreted and understood in that light.

Christmas in an African Leper Hospital and Mission
Medical missions have always played a significant role in the
expansion of Christianity. Even as Jesus went about preaching,
teaching, and healing, so his church has considered it an essential part of its ministry to heal the broken bodies, to bring sight
to the blind, hearing to the deaf — in short, to consecrate the
healing ministry to his glory. That spirit is beautifully reflected
in a brief description of the interrelationship between a mission
and a hospital:

Eyes bright with happiness, our little girl's nurse, Mujinga, put the
gift which she had just received for herself in the collection plate. It
was only twenty francs (forty cents), but for Mujinga it represented
a choice bit of meat for her Christmas dinner, which she gladly and
freely gave up.

In the nearby colony a group of lepers gave twenty-two dollars in
the Christmas offering. It represented months of hard work in the
tropical sun by people whose bodies are weakened by the dread disease and some whose limbs are no more than mere stumps.

A long row of women, full baskets of all shapes on their heads,
wind their way to the church several days before Christmas. After a
short service of thanks and praise, the baskets are taken up once
again and they all proceed to the mission hospital, where the gifts
of corn, rice, cassava, and other field produce are distributed among
the patients, Christians and non-Christians alike, many of whom are
from other tribes far away. To these non-Christians, who know only
hatred and fear, these loving gifts are an amazing manifestation of
the work of the Lord Jesus in the hearts of our Christian women and
a symbol of God's greatest Gift.

A second report reflects the vivid, transforming experience
that the gospel produces and the joyful testimony given by the
natives, generally first generation Christians.

There it was Christmas afternoon, and I was enjoying a walk
through the nearby village, only a few city blocks away from the
mission station, when I came upon a little group of people sitting
on mats on the ground and raptly listening to a miniature

"preacher" standing before them with an open Bible in his hand. With the other hand he was making the gestures which he had seen the missionary make when he stood up to preach. Strangely enough, as I squatted down behind them, only a few of them realized that I was there and turned their heads to look in my direction.

The little "preacher" was speaking of the greatest gift of all — God's Son to bring salvation and peace and joy to a sinful world. He told the old, old story most dramatically, emphasizing the poverty of Joseph and Mary and the hardships of their journey to Bethlehem, the amazing appearance of the angels to the shepherds in the cold of the night, and the still more amazing (so he said) coming of the Kings to visit the humble Child.

Abyssinia (Ethiopia)

Christmas has been celebrated in Abyssinia, or Ethiopia, as it is officially known, from earliest times. Just how far-reaching the witness of the Ethiopian eunuch mentioned in Acts 8:26 ff. may have been, as regards establishing and propagating the new faith, it seems clear that Christianity has had a continuous history in that ancient country since 330 or longer. The Coptic Church there observes Christmas not on December 25, but on January 7.

The observance of the season centers around the church. Many of the church buildings are centuries old and are hewn from rock. They are generally built square, with a court surrounding them. The altar, though usually made of wood, holds a slab or two of marble, and even more frequently of pure gold. The ark is covered with gold and precious gems.

Lalibela is known as the "Jerusalem of Ethiopia." On Christmas it is therefore crowded with pilgrims from all parts of the country. The hillsides surrounding it are literally covered and swarming with people. In the moderate climate, it is no hardship to remain outdoors all night praying and chanting, awaiting the dawn of Christmas Day.

In the morning there is a colorful procession from the church to the nearby hilltop, where the service is held according to the Coptic Church's liturgy. The procession consists of thousands of priests, monks, and nuns chanting. To keep the crowd " in line," three young men march at the head with whips, which they lash from left to right. The multitudes are fed with bread and a beverage that have been blessed by the priests.

After the worship service, the day is spent in dancing, sports, and feasting. A custom that may have little appeal to most readers is the feasting on raw meat.

Algiers

While Mohammedan mosques are almost deserted, the Catholic churches and the city take on an atmosphere of festivity. The midnight mass, almost universally observed, is celebrated here too. The governor's palace is decorated beautifully, and the streets overflow with colorful bunting. Decorations extend even to the immense docks, where steamers, ships, and small craft in the spacious harbor display prominently every flag, pennant, and piece of bunting — adding to the atmosphere of festivity. The typical French sidewalk cafés are patronized to their full capacity, and greetings are extended to friend and stranger alike.

Shopping areas are crowded and resound with the laughter and gay medley of a French street holiday.

A visitor in Algiers during the festive season reports a unique " Processional of the Pheasants " in connection with the hotel dinner. After the customary first course of soup had been served, the waiters marched in solemnly, two by two, each bearing aloft what looked like a live pheasant, set upon a silver platter. The birds looked lifelike, every feather in place, so perfectly had the taxidermist done his work. At a signal, the waiters grasped handles concealed in the backs and raised the birds off the platters, exposing the real pheasants, deliciously sauced and steaming hot.

The Congo

As in many other parts of the world, the coming of Christmas in the Congo is greeted by the singing of carols wherever the Nativity story has become known. Happy African Christians thus herald the day and later go to church, not so much to receive gifts as to give them, gifts that make it possible for others in their land to hear the glad tidings of the birth of the Savior.

Mrs. Donald F. Bobb, a missionary to Africa, gives us a vivid picture of " the light shining in the darkness " in the *Presbyterian Survey*, December, 1953, as follows:

As Kanda sat on the backless bench, his little chalk slate slid to the ground unnoticed, for he was far, far away! Each day he found it increasingly difficult to keep his mind on his schoolwork. The teacher had already looked at him rather sternly this morning, as though he knew the mind of a fourteen-year-old boy three weeks before Christmas!

There would be no lighted tree, but there was the light of God in his heart! There would be no expensive gifts, but the gift of God's love was his today and always. There would be no elaborate meal, but he would feast at the Lord's own Table. He had nothing to give his father or mother, but he had his Joy Gift tucked safely away at home in a little earthen vessel. How he had saved to make this offering on Christ's birthday!

Strains of the " Hallelujah Chorus " ran through his head. Was there ever a song so majestic, so thrilling to the heart of an African boy! Kanda had always loved to sing and knew many a hymn in its entirety from memory. When a fellow doesn't own a hymnal, he, of necessity, learns from sheer repetition.

He worked so hard on the " Hallelujah "! The missionary had played the English record, and every choir member was eager to claim this magnificent musical masterpiece for his own. It was hard work, even for those who read a little music, but Kanda, who knew no notes, had to learn his tenor part by rote. But it was worth it!

As the eventful day drew nearer, joy and expectation mounted in Kanda's heart. The night of the final rehearsal, Kanda's step was light and sure as he headed for choir practice. He didn't even wait for the second drum call, as was often his habit, but set out with the first. His heart was so full of praise and joy that he did not complain of the mile-and-a-half walk in the dark to the big church.

He was friendly and cheerful as he met smaller children and women with their babies on their hips, all scurrying along the semi-dark path to " God's House." They did not mind that they had to come night after night in order to learn the difficult songs.

Finally the "Big Night" arrived and the church was filled. Soft exclamations of "Ka! Ka!" fell from parted lips of newcomers as they beheld the once barren church now transformed by a lovely array of palms and flowers. The pageant was wonderful; the lights really did work; not too many babies cried; and Kanda tingled with joy such as he had never felt before when he stood with his two hundred African brethren singing "Hallelujah."

His father had been laughed at when he entered the school for evangelists when he was "older." Other women had mocked his mother when she enrolled in the mission school for adult women to learn to write and read God's Word. They had been faithful in teaching him all the "affairs of God."

Before the sun had risen Christmas Day, the first drum was calling, "Come to worship God; come to worship God." Every morning Kanda awoke to this drum call and went with his father and mother to the village chapel for morning prayers. This was the normal beginning of a Christian's day.

But today was special! The missionary was coming with the fascinating "magic pictures" as a special treat, and then there would be the final culmination of his Christmas — Kanda would give his Joy Gift! The only gift he had was for the Christ himself, but to Kanda this was the most natural thing in the world, for after all it was Christ's birthday. Christ *was* Christmas to this Congo boy!

Ghana, the New Republic in Africa

This new republic is viewed with keen interest politically since it may set a pattern for democracy in Africa. While not all elements in its observance of Christmas are wholesome, we shall see that the influence of the newborn King in private and in public life has wrought an amazing transformation wherever he has been received. Rev. Christian K. Agbola, a native Christian minister from this new republic, gives us a comprehensive picture, as follows:

The Christmas festival was unknown in Ghana until recently. Instead, we had yam and rice festivals and tribal dances, which are still part and parcel of our cultural life. But since the mid-nineteenth century, when the Basel, German, Swiss, and British missionaries began preaching the gospel on our soil, the Christmas celebration has become one of the most popular festivals among the people of Ghana, both Christians and non-Christians.

" Christmas," as the well-known preacher and author Charles Templeton describes it, " is the symbol of hope," the hope for the birth of Jesus Christ, our Lord and Savior. This view rightly fits that of Ghanaians about Christmas, although with additional ideas. As Christmas shopping, giving and receiving of gifts, tend to obscure the true meaning and hope of Christmas here in America, so it seems to be in Ghana. School children anxiously look forward to the presentation of their Christmas programs and expect new clothes and gifts from their parents and friends. Sweethearts and wives " sing the same tune." Grandmothers and grandfathers joyfully look forward to presents from their sons and daughters as well as from relatives at Christmas time.

In most churches in Ghana the coming of Christmas is heralded with the decoration of churches and homes with flowers and palm branches, beginning with the first Advent — that is, four weeks before Christmas. These are ways and means of heralding the coming Christmas, since we have no television as yet.

It is rather a common practice among Ghanaians to save money especially for the Christmas celebration. Those who indulge see to it that there is good wine in stock for the occasion. Groups of families buy cows, sheep, and goats to be slaughtered for Christmas Day. Chickens are confined to the coop and sometimes tied by the leg lest they escape before Christmas morning.

Christmas coincides with our main cocoa season, a time of prosperity and plenty.

One of the most wonderful occasions during the Christmas season is a day or two before Christmas. Bands of workers abroad (who probably have not seen their folks for over a year) head toward their respective homes. Some travel on foot with their suitcases or duffel bags on their heads like pilgrims. Others travel on asses or on horseback, and some by cars, trucks, and canoes. The traffic is heavy at this time. Some of these homegoers may be workers in gold and diamond mines or on farms abroad. Christmas carols and native folk songs fill the air as they journey along, and one is fully aware that Christmas is right around the corner. The trip of Mary and Joseph from Galilee to Bethlehem is now relived and made meaningful. Father Christmas (similar to Santa Claus) is also on his way, not from the North Pole, but from the jungles, to participate in the Christmas festival.

Preparations such as the rehearsal of Christmas programs, renovation and decoration of homes and streets, continue till Christmas Eve. On Christmas Eve youngsters march up and down the street with Christmas carols and shout these words: " Egbona hee, egbona hee! Egogo vo! " meaning, " Christ is coming, Christ is coming! He is near! " Fireworks get started and the streets are as bright as day.

At about seven o'clock in the evening, the church bell summons the people to church, where the Christmas tree, a fairly good-sized evergreen, or the palm tree, welcomes worshipers with bright candle light. This is quite a wonderful sight, because homes are not furnished with Christmas trees. The church is filled to capacity, and one wishes to see such a crowd in church after Christmas is over. The usual Christmas hymns are sung, and children present their programs for the evening. Most of the time the Nativity story is dramatized.

Christmas Day finds merrymaking at its highest. Early in the morning about four o'clock, a band of youngsters and older people representing the angels that sang as the shepherds were watching their flocks, sing from house to house. Families give gifts to the caroling band. In some places the caroling is done on Christmas Eve. A song like this may be heard in African, with accompaniment:

> Jesus Savior is born
> Our Lord and Savior is born,
> Good will to men, Jesus Savior is born.
> He is Lord and King,
> He's the Ruler of the World.
> Lord Jesus our Savior is born.

Christmas services are held at about 10:00 A.M. The churches are again filled to capacity. Some put on new colorful clothes of Ghana costumes, and others come in Western dress.

Feasting and dancing occupy the rest of Christmas Day. The meals consist of rice and *fufu* (a dish of yam pounded into a kind of paste), with stew or soup, porridge with bean or okra soup. Sheep, goats, cows, hogs, and chickens serve as meat for the day. Some prefer fish. Families eat together or with their neighbors and often send out food to those not invited to their homes. Gifts are distributed and everybody has a jolly good time. Enemies are reconciled, neglected correspondences are renewed, friendships that might otherwise have been completely broken are renewed. New friendships are also made, and affection between lovers is intensified. Christmas cards are sent out, especially by the literates.

The words of the Prime Minister of Ghana, Dr. Kwame Nkrumah, in his 1957 Christmas message, expressed the feeling of many a Christian in Ghana:

Christmas is a time when we naturally renew the source of our spiritual faith. Perhaps now more than ever before we would do well to turn our minds again to the teachings of Christ based upon love and forgiveness of one's enemies. It is my firm conviction that in a world divided into ideological blocks, feverishly arming for mutual annihilation with atomic and hydrogen bombs and intercontinental missiles, this is the only hope for mankind. It is certainly a world far removed from the conditions which could be achieved by following the teachings of Christ.

Liberia

In this country, on the West Coast of Africa, the Christmas message has been received through mission schools. Boys and girls studying there save their " irons," the native currency, for their Christmas offering and shopping. Beads and sugar are at the top of their list; peanuts, cooked beans, palm oil, parched rice, and salt follow.

For their tree, a beautiful oil palm with the long trunk cut off, is dragged to the dining room and decorated mainly with beautiful red bells. Throughout the buildings, palms and ferns are used for decorating.

Christmas dawn is announced at the girls' school by the singing of " Silent Night! Holy Night! " and as the carol ceases, the sound of far-off voices from across the river indicates that the boys, too, are awake and beginning to celebrate. After prayers and breakfast, the gifts are distributed. Each girl gets a new pan to eat out of, a piece of cotton cloth for a dress, a piece of perfumed soap, and some candy. Sometimes there are dolls or hand-kerchiefs sent from America. Pencils, tablets, and books are always welcomed.

After the boys have had a service, they come with their teachers to the program at the girls' school. The Christmas scene is presented, with a box full of excelsior for the manger, Mary in a sheet, and Joseph in a gown of native cloth. Singing and recitations constitute the rest of the program.

Then follows the dinner, which is eaten out of doors. All sit in a circle on the grass, using their new pans. Each enjoys a generous portion of rice, a good piece of beef, and two cookies. Candy is eaten slowly since there is not much of it. Games follow the dinner, and at dusk all wait for the most spectacular event of the day — the fireworks. The children shout and gasp with delight, content to go to bed only when the last golden spark has disappeared.

Now Christmas is over, unless a steamer puffing up the river during the next few days should bring a belated box of gifts from friends. But now there are letters of thanks to write, causing the spirit of joy and thanksgiving to linger on.

The Union of South Africa

In South Africa, as we observe in other areas, we have to keep in mind the three groups — the unchristianized natives, the immigrant peoples with their Christian background, and the younger churches among the natives.

Christmas in the Union of South Africa is a summer holiday. For most people it is an out-of-town day. In December, the southern summer brings glorious days of sunshine that carry an irresistible invitation to the beaches, the rivers, and the shaded mountain slopes. Then the South African holiday season reaches its height. Schools are closed for the long summer vacations, and camping is the order of the day. If South Africa has no snow at Christmas, it has flowers, many beautiful varieties of cultivated and wild flowers which being in their full pride seem to flame as brightly as a yule-log fire.

In many ways South Africans cling to the Christmas customs

of the Old World. Shop windows are draped with sparkling cotton wool and tinsel to give the traditional Christmassy setting familiar to shoppers in London and New York. Even Father Christmas, a South African prototype of Saint Nicholas or Santa Claus, braves the sunny side of the street in his customary robes — cloak and hood trimmed with cotton wool to simulate snow — and points the way to the elaborate "toylands" in the big stores. In the shops he is seen helping parents to choose their gifts and spreading fun among the children.

Christmas greeting cards, complete with robin and snow-decked cottages, are exchanged during the season. In the cities and towns, carol singers make their rounds on Christmas Eve. Church services are held on Christmas morning. Christmas Eve celebrations in larger centers include "carols by candlelight" and special screen and floor shows.

Homes are lavishly decorated, usually with pine branches, and all have the decorated Christmas fir tree in a corner, with presents for the children under it. Holly is missing, as none grows in the warm South African climate. Sometimes a local type of mistletoe is hung up in a strategic position, but more often imitation mistletoe has to do. At bedtime on Christmas Eve, children may also hang up their stockings for presents from Father Christmas.

Some streets are colorfully lighted at night, with floodlights on prominent buildings and a sparkling Christmas tree on the city square.

For many South Africans, Christmas dinner is an open-air lunch. For many more it is the traditional dinner of either turkey, roast beef, mince pies, or suckling pig, yellow rice (turmeric) with raisins, vegetables, and plum pudding, crackers, paper hats, and all. In the afternoon families go out into the country, and usually there are games or bathing in the warm sunshine and then they return home for the cool of the evening. Boxing Day is also a proclaimed public holiday usually spent in the open air. It falls on December 26 and is a day of real relaxation.

For the non-European races of South Africa, Christmas is a

holiday, a day of good eating and of lively exchange and enjoyment of gifts. On Christmas Day the colored natives of the
Cape commence their week-long carnival of singing, dancing,
and parading the streets with pipe and string bands, dressed in
their gay and fanciful costumes.

7. Christmas in the Middle East

FROM Bethlehem the events that constitute the essence of Christmas have come, and in Bethlehem they have not been forgotten during the twenty centuries that have passed. They have been and are being commemorated there and elsewhere in varied forms; but the little town of Bethlehem has not only exerted the world-wide influence we have noted in previous chapters as regards the far-reaching transformation that the birth of Jesus has wrought, but it also continues to cause the hearts of men each recurring season to look unto it and ponder anew the things that came to pass there.

A few people from every country join the throng of native Christians, in this otherwise insignificant city, at Christmas time. Millions hear the church bells send out their Christmas message over the ether waves from Bethlehem to the ends of the earth. While it is regrettable that the Holy Land itself and the neighboring countries that have come to be designated the Near East in recent years have failed to receive the Prince of Peace as regards the great majority of the population, he does have in each of these countries those who turn, not to Mecca or Medina, as do the Moslems, but to the City of the Nativity, which has come to be a holy place for Christians of both East-ern and Western churches.

Arabia — a Christmas in the Desert

Saudi Arabia may be said to be completely Moslem. No church spire raises its cross. The only public places of worship are the domed mosques. More than that, those who settle there, even temporarily, must abide by the laws of the country as regards, for example, the manufacture, importation, and sale of alcoholic beverages. From the restrictions imposed on worship we can immediately conclude that there is no Christmas among the Arabs as a people.

However, here as in many other countries, there are large foreign settlements. In this case there is a community of some five thousand in Dhahran, employees of the Aramco Oil Company, the largest permanent colony outside of the United States. Within such a settlement there is usually practically complete liberty as to religious observances in houses and recreation halls.

Dorothy Thompson, in the December, 1957, issue of the *Ladies' Home Journal*, reports concerning this settlement's manner of Christmas celebration. They worship at altars in homes or in the recreation center, whether Protestant or Catholic. Having imported Christmas foods and decorations from the homeland, being so far from home, they enter into the preparation for Christmas with all the greater zest. Wreaths of marigolds and other annuals that bloom there in December are used to decorate the doors. Colored lights beautify the houses. Christmas carols resound through the open windows.

There is, quite naturally, even more visiting from home to home than in the United States, also from club to club. When Christmas packages from home are delayed, cartons of cigarettes beautifully wrapped or a box of home-baked cookies take their place.

At times the Moslems, too, catch the infection and accompany a warm handshake with a " Merry Christmas."

The presentation of the Nativity through narration and song

is skillfully done. Voices narrate the sacred stories from Luke and Matthew, the shepherds appear with their sheep, shawls over their shoulders and carrying their familiar shepherd crooks. Angels appear over the Lord's birthplace (manger or cradle), and a chorus joins them in " Joy to the World." This is followed by " O Come, All Ye Faithful," " O Little Town of Bethlehem," " Silent Night! Holy Night! " and other songs.

People in such settlements learn to know that the story of Christmas is not centered at the North Pole; neither is it native to Europe, nor the New World; but its home, as far as geographical location is concerned, is the Near East, from which it went forth into all the world to become a universal religion, including all mankind — ecumenical, as we frequently say today.

Armenia (Old Armenia)

Only the Armenians, of the Eastern people, cling to the ancient custom of observing Christmas on January 18.

One week before Christmas all the villagers fast by not eating animal food, and on the last day they eat no food at all. On Christmas Eve they attend Communion. After the service they return to their homes; the women light the house, and the time has come when the fast is to be broken. This is generally done with a dish called *Pilav*, a rice food. The children go in groups to the housetops and hang their handkerchiefs over the roofs and sing,

> Rejoice and be glad
> Open your bag
> And fill our handkerchiefs
> Hallelujah! Hallelujah!

The people in the house fill their handkerchiefs with raisins and fried wheat or tie some money into them.

Shredded chicken breast cooked with wheat, cinnamon, and olive oil is a popular Christmas dinner dish. Armenian swains give their girls trays of cakes, eggs, raisins, and sweetmeats.

In the course of the evening the priest visits the homes of

mourning in his parish and offers a prayer for the souls of the dead and words of comfort for the living.

On Christmas Day all villagers hasten to the morning church services. At this time the ceremony of pouring out the Holy Oil of Baptism takes place. Glasses are dipped into the blessed water. Some of them take water home to mix with the pure earth (Earth of the Holy Oil) for special blessings.

During Christmas week young men and women greet each other with: " Happy blessing-of-the-water to you. May you live to see the Holy Resurrection." And the proper response is, " With you together let the blessing of the Holy Oil of Baptism be on your house."

A poem often recited in this season expresses a beautiful sentiment:

> The lips of the Christ-child are like to twin leaves;
> They let roses fall when he smiles tenderly.
> The tears of the Christ-child are pearls when he grieves;
> The eyes of the Christ-child are deep as the sea.
> Like pomegranate grains are the dimples he hath,
> And clustering lilies spring up in his path!

India

The story of an original Christmas tree indicates the marvelous manner in which the spirit of the season finds new ways of expressing the joyous message from Bethlehem's plains. On the plains of India no pines nor cedars, in fact no conifers, grow. So the natives with the help of a missionary devised a unique plan of producing a Christmas tree.

Out in the *kothar* (the place where grain is stacked and threshed), there was a big pile of rice straw. A bundle was made, as tall as a small man; then ropes were twisted, also of the straw, and wound around the bundle. The next day " branches " were put in, made in the same way; then the whole " tree " was soaked in water and carried into the church and there thickly plastered with mud. On the next day, Christmas Day, green twigs of a species of oleander were stuck in, close together, and candles put on the ends of the " branches " and on the top of the tree. The trimmings were simple as could be — paper chains, and mica, scattered over the trees. Hardly could any decorator in a fashionable church at home have been more proud of his achievements than were Samsun and Dudru, two men who had grown from boyhood to manhood under the tutelage of a Christian missionary.

In the evening for the celebration, candles were placed into mud candleholders and set in all the church windows and on the backs of the benches, for there are no lamps in the church. Many of the houses of worship are plain brick buildings, plastered with mortar and whitewashed, with mud floors and a few benches down the center. The windows are often of cloth, and the bell is not in the tower but in front of the church. Everything is very simple, as is all of life with the Christians in India.

In the mountainous regions evergreen trees can be obtained more conveniently, but it is doubtful whether they provide as much joy as the services that center around such trees as those described above. In church, mission schools, and benevolent institutions as well as in homes, the children participate with songs and recitations. Native Christians sing songs written by themselves and set to their own music accompanied by native instruments; series of pantomimes are enacted presenting the Scripture scenes.

Miss Mable Hamilton, missionary to India, sent us this vivid account of " Christmas at Village No. 190 " in the year 1945:

This particular Christmas Day we had planned to go to Village No. 190, for we always spend Christmas in some village with the Indian people. We all looked forward to these occasions because the Indians love to celebrate, and we equally enjoy joining in with the festivities.

> The bear went over the mountain
> To see what he could see.

Early this morning the town band was lined up in front of the house, playing that tune for all it was worth. Of course, " I'm

Dreaming of a White Christmas" might have been a little more appropriate number for the yuletide season, but since none of the band had ever seen a "White Christmas," and did not even know the words to the tune they were playing, it made little difference to them. To them it was music. Every man played by ear, and each instrument played the melody. "The Bear Went Over the Mountain" and "Yankee Doodle" were the latest song hits and were played without discrimination at Christmas, religious feasts, weddings, and funerals alike. The band was composed of non-Christians for whom the true meaning of Christmas had not dawned. To them it was just another British-declared holiday, and of course everyone likes a holiday.

Soon we were on our way to the village. As we neared it, and the sound of our engine came within hearing distance, we could see all the boys and girls pouring out of their homes. They always lined up in the most strategic places along the road so they could jump on the back of the car.

After meeting and talking with the people of the village and visiting the sick, we walked to the church. The building and grounds were decorated with multicolored streamers and banners strung from one end of the church to the other. The periodic outbursts of rockets, flares, and firecrackers gave atmosphere to the festivities.

The service, we had been told, would begin promptly at ten, but we have learned by experience that time means little to the village farmer. They would do well to begin by twelve, so we had not broken any speed limits getting to the village.

Soon the people started gathering. All were dressed in their finest. Everyone who could afford it had on a suit of new clothes — a custom very similar to the one many Americans observe at Easter. It was truly a colorful sight. The Indians love color, and according to their taste, a bright red and bright pink is as pretty a combination as can be had.

Before long the church was filled to overflowing. The Christmas service is the best attended of the year. All sat on the floor of the neatly built mud-brick church, the women and children on one side and the men on the other. Of course, the women have no maids with whom to leave their children at home, so they are all brought to church and here is where the confusion always begins. That day as Father began his sermon, he was soon offered competition by one, then two, then more sqaulling babies, by women talking out, and by one little rascal trying to untie his shoestrings. Through all this Father patiently told them of Jesus and of our hope of salvation, made possible through this Savior whose birth we are celebrating. After the service, candy and oranges were passed out to all the children.

One of the elders had invited us to eat dinner in his home. The meal was truly a feast prepared in the best of Indian style. On the way, Mother gathered us children together for her usual " pre-village-meal " lecture. We must not drink any water except our boiled water brought from home. We were to be nice to, but not play with, any of the children with sore eyes or sores. And above all, we were not to eat too much of the food that contained hot peppers. She knew our weakness.

It would be lacking in manners if an Indian guest failed to belch loudly after a meal to show his appreciation, so when we had finished, my brothers, not wishing to appear ungrateful, proceeded to try to carry out this to the best of their ability, possibly more for the purpose of embarrassing Mother and Father and antagonizing their sisters than of pleasing the host.

The rest of the day was spent in watching the athletic part of the Christmas Day celebrations. This consisted of track races, games, medley relays, and especially wrestling matches.

That happy day had fast drawn to a close. After many fond good-byes, we started home. As soon as we arrived, we rushed up on the high flat roof of our house and lighted the little candles which we placed all along the roof. This is the custom among Indian Christians on Christmas night. After we had finished, we stood, looking out, seeing the home of each Indian Christian outlined, as it were, with little twinkling stars, and we felt that it was a truly impressive sight. There in the cool stillness of that Christmas night, the second part of the angels' message came to mind, " Peace on earth, good will to men."

Few of us, if any, will ever know firsthand what it means to be a patient in a leper hospital or even what joy there is in bringing new hope to leper patients. A little glimpse of what both of them mean comes to us in a letter from Lois M. Marsilje, dated 1955, which we may well entitle " A Leper Mission Christmas."

Last year the Christmas season was ushered in by a trip to one of the nearby villages where some of the hospital staff joined in the traditional hoisting of the Christmas flag. This is an interesting custom practiced in most of the villages about a month before Christmas or early in December. The Christians gather together about the Christmas flag as it is raised high on an extended bamboo pole, to remain thus, a reminder to Hindu and Christian alike, of the real meaning of Christmas. The Christmas flag is a white banner with a red cross in the center, a cross for the child who was born to die. On this occasion Dr. Julius Savarirayan spoke on the wonder of the incarnation when Christ came into the world to show man what God was like — and that, of course, was climaxed and completed only in the cross.

The Sunday before Christmas the hospital Christian Endeavor Society took the Christmas message and their white gifts to a village, as is their usual custom. We rode the fifteen miles to the village by bus and car, singing carols in the various languages of the group as we rode along. After alighting from the bus, we paddled through the streams flowing in the otherwise dry river bed. I had to remove shoes and stockings and go barefoot along with the others, much to their delight.

The villagers had gathered and were ready for us by the time we arrived. They listened attentively to the Christmas message as presented by one of the nurses, and even more attentively when a student nurse, with the aid of the flannelgraph, told the message of God's love, first as exemplified in the story of the prodigal son, and then as culminating in the greatest gift of all, God's only Son, Jesus Christ, the gift of Christmas.

After the service, the gifts to the Christian and Hindu children were distributed — slates and pencils for the younger children; notebooks, combs, and hair ribbons for the older children; and some articles of clothing for each child. Some were in rags and almost naked as they went up to receive their welcome gift. These gifts had been donated by the Christian Endeavor members, some in kind, and some in money, taken from their small salaries or stipends. This is, for the nurses, the great occasion of the year to which they all look forward with anticipation. Families also received enough rice for a family Christmas meal, a tin of powdered milk, and for each member a special treat of a banana and a cupful of puffed rice which they eat as we would popcorn.

Christmas Day was spent much as in other years, beginning with early morning caroling through the wards of the hospital; breakfast together with the nurses; giving of cards, tracts, and candy to all the patients; at noon Christmas dinner with the nurses, after which they received their Christmas presents; games and sports for the children and members of the congregation in the afternoon.

Christmas came late to the leprosy patients, two weeks after Christmas Day. That day there was an unusually large clinic, 535 leprosy patients. After receiving his medicine, each patient presented his registration slip and received a Christmas tract, explaining the meaning of the day. For these patients we had especially selected those cards which had the Christmas picture, especially those showing the baby Jesus, which was particularly requested by so many. The children received plaques, made and sent by one of the missionary organizations in the U.S.A. Once these were seen, many asked for one of the " glass pictures " as they called them. One old patient, a former soldier, came to me, saluted, and then proudly displayed six cards which he had received the six previous years, all carefully preserved and remarkably clean. This simple gift is appreciated.

When I was taking pictures of the group of leprosy patients, one educated Brahman patient asked me to take a picture of him as an example of one who had been cured by our treatment. He is a violinist who could no longer play his violin because of deformed and weakened fingers. But now he can play again and can return as a respected member to his community. He wants friends in the U.S.A. to know how they have helped him.

The Christmas tracts were also appreciated. Scattered about the grounds near the clinic building were little groups of patients, looking at their pictures and reading their tracts. One man was so interested in his reading that he scarcely noticed when I took a picture of him. But the supply of tracts ran out before the end of the clinic, and I had to explain, " I am sorry; there are no more tracts this week " to the repeated requests for " pictures with reading." Hearts are hungry for the message of Christmas, the message of God who loved man so much that he stooped to come to him as a weak and helpless babe and lived among men as one like them, yet as their Lord and Master. We know not what fruit the Spirit may bring from the reading of this wondrous message.

Last Christmas has come and long since gone, but the message of peace and good will to men lingers on from year to year, and now another Christmas season is approaching. May the spirit of the Christ-child fill our hearts and bring true peace and joy.

Iran (Persia)

Tradition claims Iran as the home of the Magi, men who studied the stars, thus being led to follow the star " till it came and stood over where the young child was."

Christmas in Iran is known as the Little Feast, Easter being considered the Great Feast. The first twenty-five days of December are a fast for the Christians of Persia, a period during which no meat, eggs, milk, or cheese are eaten.

Christmas Eve is the last day of the fast. After the early mass, at dawn of Christmas morning, the people are permitted to break fast and the festivities begin. A popular dish is *harasa* (a chicken stew). This is cooked in sufficient quantities to last several days.

Santa Claus is unknown here, and while there is no exchange of presents, the children generally receive new clothes which they proudly wear during the festive days.

Iraq

While most of the people of Iraq (or Irak) are Moslems, there are also both old and younger Christian churches there.

The older churches very largely are of the Coptic group (see Abyssinia), having a fairly continuous history from the early Christian centuries on. Though having preserved the heart of the gospel, they have also accumulated some superstitious practices, several of which appear in their Christmas observances.

On Christmas Eve the family gather in the courtyard, and one of the children reads the story of the Nativity from an Arabic Bible while the members of the family hold lighted candles. After the reading, a bonfire of dried thorns is lighted in a corner of the courtyard. If all the thorns burn to ashes, it means good fortune for the family. When the thorns have been reduced to ashes, each one jumps over the ashes three times and makes a wish.

On Christmas Day a similar fire is lighted in the church while the congregation chants a hymn. Then follows a procession in which the Bishop carries an image of the infant Jesus on a scarlet cushion. The service ends with the Bishop's reaching forth and touching a member of the congregation; he in turn touches the next one, and this continues until all have received " The Touch of Peace."

Among the younger churches, Protestant missions largely, the children crowd the meeting hall to participate in the Christmas program. They generally have learned " Joy to the World " and have heard the stories of the shepherds and the Wise Men. Colored filmstrips or movies serve to clarify the stories and to impress them more deeply.

During the festive season there is much visiting in the homes. The patients in the hospital, the high school students, the women in their society meetings, the workers in the homes, workers from other countries engaged in building and industrial projects — all join in the good will that flows from fellowshiping around a cup of tea or coffee.

Israel (Palestine)

Although each of the best-known cities of the Holy Land brings to mind sacred associations with New Testament events — Bethlehem, Nazareth, and Jerusalem — it is to Bethlehem that we turn most naturally on Christmas Eve. In Jerusalem, the majority of the population is of the Mohammedan and Jewish faiths, considerably less than one sixth being Christian. Nazareth has its appeal as we recall the synagogue that Jesus may have attended while growing up and where he began his public ministry. We remember his wondrous words and his mighty works at Capernaum, Bethsaida, and other cities bordering on the Sea of Galilee. But the urge comes to Christians in December, " Let us go even unto Bethlehem and see this thing that has happened."

If we were to go literally to observe Christmas in the land where it originated, we would have to plan carefully as to the date, for it is celebrated there at three different times. The Roman Catholics and the Protestants observe December 25; the Greek Orthodox, Syrians, and Abyssinians, January 6, which is the Feast of the Epiphany; the Armenians, January 18, which is January 6, old-style calendar. It becomes clearer to us when we remember that, while Europe and its colonies and the Americas follow the Roman calendar, the Greek Church still uses the Julian.

To understand the total picture of Christmas observances in and around Bethlehem, it is necessary to remember the mixed religious complexion of Palestine. The majority, of course, are Jews and Moslems (Arabs). Of the Christian population, the largest group is Roman Catholic, which includes those of the Armenian rite, the Latin rite, and those who acknowledge spiritual allegiance to the See of Rome. The next largest group is the Greek Orthodox, which gives its allegiance to the Greek Patriarch of Jerusalem. The smaller groups of native Christians are the independent Armenians and the Copts, the latter being related to the early sect in Egypt by that name. In addition, there are the Protestant colonies, represented by the Anglicans and the German Lutherans.

Although the customary carol-singing on Bethlehem Square is provided by the Protestant Mission, the midnight mass on Christmas Eve, January 6, and January 18, held in the Church of the Nativity by the Roman Catholics, the Greek Catholics, and the Armenian Christians, respectively, quite naturally attracts vast numbers, both of the native Christians and of the sojourners and special visitors who have come to spend one Christmas Eve in "the little town of Bethlehem." This church supposedly was built over the exact place where Jesus was born.

Two places attract pilgrims in the Christmas season in the Holy Land: the Church of the Nativity and the Shepherds' Fields, possibly a mile or two outside the city.

Although the Eastern Orthodox Church has its celebration of the birth of our Lord thirteen days after the Western churches, there is much excitement among Roman Catholics and Protestants in the Holy Land on Christmas Eve, particularly in Jerusalem and even more in Bethlehem At about nine o'clock in the evening, buses, private cars, and taxis carry large numbers of people from Jerusalem and other nearby towns to the city of Jesus' birth. Many excited groups walk the six miles that separate Jerusalem from Bethlehem.

Observe some of the pilgrims. Here is a Bethlehem woman in her picturesque costume which is so distinctive that a Bethlehem woman is recognized anywhere in the country. She comes, and stooping over, kisses the holy spot. Yonder is a Christian peasant from the east country. Her long, black robes drag on the ground as she comes down the stairs. She too leans over, and her tattooed lips reverently touch the place where she believes Jesus was born. In back of her is a woman dressed in the very height of the fashion of a European capital, but her lips touch the same honored spot with great reverence. The men come — old and young, Eastern and Western — and all obey the urge to kiss the spot where they believe the Son of God became man. Some who are Protestants do not kiss this center of attraction, but they too experience a feeling of awe. Everybody moves on, because other hundreds are waiting for an opportunity to pay homage to a place, *the* place where Jesus reputedly was born, over which there has been erected the Church of the Nativity. According to some, it dates back as far as Constantine, 330; but more likely, it was built in the days of Justinian, who ruled from 527 to 565. The nave of the church belongs to the Roman Catholic, Greek Orthodox, and Armenian churches, each of which has a separate nearby convent. Below the floor and approached by two staircases is the cave of the Nativity. A silver star in the pavement indicates the supposed spot where our Lord was born. Around it is the inscription, *Hic de Virgine Maria Jesus Christus natus est* ("Here of the Virgin Mary, Jesus Christ was born"). Above this spot are fifteen silver lamps, kept perpetually burning. Six of these belong to the Greek Orthodox, five to the Armenians, and four to the Roman Catholics. War would ensue if one were to be removed or another to be added. The *status quo* must be maintained.

The main entrance to this edifice, so small that only one can enter at a time and must stoop in so doing, is made so because of fear of mob trouble. Moslems, at one time, are supposed to have entered the church on horseback. Either Moslems or antagonistic Christian groups might attempt to storm the place during intense religious excitement were it otherwise. Police and guards watch closely all the events of the Christmas Eve gathering and are prepared for anything that might happen.

Take note, as we proceed, that the place of birth, the manger, and the adoration are all supposed to be in the chapel of the Church of the Nativity. The mass begins at midnight and continues for an hour and a half. A trained choir of monks sings the service. At various points in the program a bishop removes one gorgeous robe from the patriarch, the head of the Roman Catholic Church in the country, and puts on him another one even more beautiful. This is repeated from time to time until the close of the service.

The church is crowded. Fortunate ones who came early have seats, and others are mulling about through the aisles as the Latin service continues. At its close the aged patriarch takes the life-size image of the Christ from the high altar and leads a procession through the church and down into the grotto. The bells chime as the robed ecclesiastic places the image in a manger, where it is to lie until Epiphany, January 6, the day when several of the Eastern churches send representatives to the church to celebrate their Christmas.

So the service ends, and buses and cars carry the weary spectators back to their homes. For the ones who walk, there is more than an hour of hilly travel ahead for them. Many of the worshipers remain in Bethlehem to see the dawn come over the hills across which the Wise Men traveled some time after that Holy Night, guided by a star, to present the infant Jesus with gold, frankincense, and myrrh.

But not all spend time in the church with the crowds, the music, the noise, and the excitement. Other large groups can be seen leaving the town and walking out along a country road, possibly carrying lanterns or flashlights, irresistibly drawn to the

Shepherds' Fields. Probably there is no reason to suppose that these special fields witnessed that strange phenomenon when angels announced to the simple pious folk who were watching over the animals intended for the Temple sacrifice that " Unto you is born this day in the city of David a Savior, which is Christ the Lord." But whether they be the very fields or not, the event occurred in this vicinity. Here there is nothing tawdry. There are no officials in special dress. It is a group of simple folk who meet under the stars in the fields outside the town. We hear the bells of Bethlehem ring across the space. Far away in the distance we can see the automobile lights on the Jerusalem road, with the late-comers to the pageant. On the hillsides around the town, as on that eventful night so long ago, sheep still graze and find shelter in the sheepfolds. The shepherds still are serving under the stars, bathed in the significant stillness. The scene still reflects the peaceful simplicity of the first Christmas Eve.

Here is peace. All speak in subdued voices. The starry firmament above and the significant event associated with these scenes fills all with awe and reverence. They speak in subdued voices. Germans, Scandinavians, English, Armenians, Arabs, Hebrews, Christians, Americans, and others find people of like minds, waiting for still others to gather.

Lebanon

This country, to the north of Israel, is often referred to as the Christian State of Lebanon because of the remarkable development in the direction of tolerance and cultural standards that Christianity and Western influence have developed there.

To the Consulate General of Lebanon in New York, we owe a very vivid and complete description of " Christmas in a Lebanon Village," by Ibn El-Khoury:

The village in Lebanon from which I came is situated midway between the summit and the base of the mountain. It is near enough to the city of Beirut to be in partial touch with modernizing influences, and far enough to retain traces of the old color of the patri-archal, simple life of the hardy mountaineers. The church, for in-stance, had benches for seating worshipers, a privilege and a luxury enjoyed by only a few of the churches of the more pretentious mountain villages. Yet the latticed partition separating the men's from the women's quarters remained, as also all the rituals as prac-ticed for centuries in the old Syriac language in the full grandeur of their simplicity.

Next to Easter, which by virtue of the fact that it falls in the full bloom of spring and following a long period of penitence which, during Lent, is practiced even now in those sequestered Lebanon villages as it was in the earliest periods of Christianity — next to Easter, Christmas is the festal day observed with the greatest display of ostentation and exhilaration. It is for the Lebanese Christians, not a day of exchange of presents, because, for some reason or other, presents to children are given on New Year's Day, but an occasion for real spiritual joy and elation to which the mountain folks deliver themselves with all the purity of their unsophisticated minds. The atmosphere along about this season seems to be impregnated with the fragrance of the lofty virtues symbolized by the birth of Christ, and the villagers in their transports of ecstasy seem all to be living in a charmed world of their own.

Preparations for Christmas festivities are conducted on quite an elaborate scale. Every household in the village, from that of the sheik or magistrate, down to that of the humblest farmer or goat herder, as the day approaches, vibrates more and more with the spirit of activity. *Baklawa, burma, mulabbas*, and other sweets are ordered from the city to be served to visitors, while the native prod-ucts such as dried figs, raisins, and pickles are always within easy reach. Most important of all is the testing and sampling of wine. Wine, the genuine fermented juice of the grape, the national drink of Lebanon, the fluid which inspires the village bards and is from time immemorial the first and foremost token of proffered hospital-ity, must of necessity lead the list of festal preparations. The vintage of the preceding crop is therefore sampled as safely as possible be-fore Christmas, and when anyone finds that his wine has not suffi-ciently aged to suit the fastidious taste of a connoisseur — and they are all connoisseurs of wine in Mt. Lebanon — he borrows a jar of older wine from his neighbor, for only the best must be served on Christmas.

Of a more complex nature are the activities to be observed in the rectory of the priest. His family, to be sure, looks forward to the advent of Christmas with as much anticipation of joy as any household in the village. For the priests of the Eastern Churches, especially parish priests, are married. This privilege is enjoyed not only by adherents of the Greek Orthodox Church, which is independent of Rome, but by priests of the Greek Melchite and Maronite Churches, which are both integral branches of the Church of Rome, as well. And in some instances the priest can boast of larger families than any of the most ambitious laymen among the villagers.

But the *khouriat,* or the priest's wife, has more to look after than the ordinary matron, and the children of the *khoury* are called upon to do more than prepare their holiday costumes and make necessary arrangements for the reception and entertainment of guests and callers. I happen to be the son of a priest and I know. My recollection of these circumstances, although dating back to more than a quarter century, is still as vivid and clear as if I had witnessed this procession of incidents only yesterday. Rather, it is perhaps now that I begin to appreciate the exquisite romance that is so closely interwoven with the life of a Lebanon villager, now that I have come to experience the dull routine, the driving urge, the mad rush of life in an American city.

Christmas Eve is spent either in silent meditation or in open prayer almost in every house, members of the family crowding around the open fire awaiting the coming of midnight to answer the call of the church bell beckoning them to come to mass. No food in any form is taken from the hour of sunset because almost everyone receives Communion. But all the good things to eat and to drink are already prepared and placed within convenient reach for the festivities that are to follow.

At the stroke of midnight the church bell begins to peal out its cheerful tidings of the day commemorating the birth of the Lord. Long and methodical are these silvery sounds that fill the air with their message of joy and are echoed throughout the sleeping valleys of the mountain. At times a weird, soul-stirring effect is produced by the conflict of sound coming from the varied rings of the different-sized bells of several churches in the same village, or of neighboring villages within hearing distance. This prelude to the Christmas festivities is one of their outstanding features, because it is for the young men of each village a test of strength and endurance, also calling for no little amount of skill in producing the different combinations of bell play. In most churches, the belfry is raised about midway in the length of the building over the side wall close to one of the center doors. There the pretentious young men gather around the dangling rope, in full view of the worshipers, to take turns at performing the feat. We may be sure that while this is proceeding, many pairs of admiring eyes are peering through the latticed partition focusing on the knot of competing young men gathered around the bell rope. This is kept up until the whole congregation is in church and the services actually begin.

The midnight mass is a sacred institution in the Christian villages of Lebanon. Rain or snow or dry weather, attendance is compulsory. There seems to be associated with these midnight services in the minds of these sincere, devout Christians special graces hallowed by centuries of observance. To miss being in church with the birth of the new day heralding anew the birth of Christ is a calamity.

The service progresses very slowly, and as the reading of the Gospel approaches, a man is seen to rise and walk to the rear of the church where, at the door of the latticed partition, he takes from the arms of a woman an infant apparently but a few months old. He carries it gently to the altar landing and, as the priest faces the worshipers, he beckons the man to approach. The priest rests the Holy Book on the head of the child and reads the Gospel from that position. This reverential action is supposed to carry with it a special blessing.

Toward the end of the mass the men begin to line up along the altar railing to receive Communion, but the women form in line within their own partition and the priest descends the steps of the altar and walks slowly down the center aisle, preceded by acolytes bearing lighted candles and all the while burning incense, to meet them at that location.

Christmas is the feast of peace on earth and good will toward men, and in these primitive Christian churches in Lebanon villages a physical interpretation is given to these symbolic words. At the time the officiating priest announces the words of the angels, toward the conclusion of the mass, he touches the outstretched hand of the acolyte to his right, and the latter immediately rises and passes the *salaam*, or peace token, by the touch of hand, to the first man next to the altar. The *salaam* is then passed in like manner from the one to the other until it goes the full round of the church. By now the hour has well advanced toward dawn, and the church begins to pour out its stream of humanity from the different exits only to form in little groups in the open court of the church to exchange greetings. Presently small bands of joyful men and women form and are seen traveling in different directions. The infant Christ has come again to announce peace and good will, and now the happy, leisurely villagers invoke all means at their command to accentuate and radiate this good feeling.

Pakistan

In this predominantly Moslem country, there are nevertheless over one half million Christians who celebrate Christmas in many ways similar to our Christmas, especially in regard to worship and family festivities.

Through the Pakistan Mission to the United Nations, we received an excellent description of " Christmas in Pakistan " by the Rev. Inayat Masih:

The business community in the larger shopping centers of the big cities, regardless of religious belief, features window displays, colored lights, and many of the attractions that are synonymous with Western Christmas shopping. Restaurants feature Christmas puddings and other traditional dishes on their menus for the holiday.

As anywhere in the Christian world, Christmas in Pakistan is a time for the gathering together of families. Children's parties are held in the parishes at which the traditional Santa Claus makes his appearance and distributes presents to the children. On Christmas Eve, churches and Christian homes are illuminated, and at midnight the joyous peals of the church bells mark the beginning of Christmas Day. There is midnight worship in most of the churches.

Holiday decorations, the singing of carols, and other festivities are governed by family traditions and are not common to all parts of Pakistan. Many non-Christians, however, send Christmas cards and gifts to their Christian friends during the season.

The village Christian community, which is by far the largest Christian community in Pakistan, generally holds Christmas services in a decorated open-air compound in the village — the church, if there is one, is generally too small to accommodate the large crowd of worshipers who gather together — in many cases from different villages. In the cities, the poor are not forgotten, and most congregations provide food or other remembrances for needy families.

Christmas celebrations in many of the great churches and cathedrals in cities are broadcast over Radio Pakistan, thus bringing the services, with the ringing of the Christmas chimes and the choirs singing carols, into homes throughout Pakistan.

Since the birthday anniversary of the founder of Pakistan, Quaid-i-Azam Mohammed Ali Jinnah, falls on December 25, Pakistanis on this national holiday have still further cause for festivities and rejoicing during the Christian Christmas season, and the foreign visitor has an impression that the whole country is in a mood of celebration.

Above all, in Pakistan, as all over the world, Christmas is a family festival. Every Pakistani child loves the time and considers it most enjoyable when his loved ones are together on the Holy Day.

Syria

The holiday season in Syria differs considerably from that in most other countries. It begins on Saint Barbara's Day, December 4, and continues until Epiphany, January 6. Saint Barbara was outstanding in goodness, so that her faith and love made her an example to the children. On this eve, sacred to her memory, a table of sweetmeats is arranged, prepared from nuts, sugar, honey, and wheat, the latter in memory of the dead and signifying the resurrection of the soul. Little children are taught lessons of unselfishness and thoughtfulness for the less fortunate. A prosperous family will help several others into which sorrow and poverty have come. To homes in which loved ones have passed away, sweetmeats are sent, and to the houses of the poor the children bring their cakes with the greeting: "May God bless you and bring you happiness every year. Father and Mother beg you to accept these gifts from us." At a social hour of dancing, singing, and games, wheat is cooked and flavored with sugar, rose water, and candy. The girls at the party, as a sign that they have learned the lesson of the good Saint Barbara, come one by one to an elderly woman who anoints their eyes with a salve. The above will be clearer if we quote completely the story of Saint Barbara as it has been translated:

> Barbara, the saint, was elected of God.
> She gave her bread to the poor.
> Her miserly father rebuked her
> And threatened her with his sword.
> When he caught her with the bread in her lap
> She cried unto God in her fear.
> God turned the sword in her father's hand
> Into a crochet needle.
> When her father demanded to see
> What she concealed in her lap,
> She cried unto God for help
> And the bread in her lap turned to roses.

On December 6, a special mass is said in the churches for Saint Nicholas Thaumaturgus, the Wonder-Worker. The stories that have gathered around him relate him to our modern Santa Claus.

On Christmas Eve, as many as can do so, join the pilgrimage to Bethlehem, participating in the services described above, under " Israel." In each Syrian church on Christmas Eve a bonfire of vine stems is made in the middle of the church in honor of the Magi who were cold from their long journey. Home from the mass, the father tells the story of the Christ-child, and all join in singing Christmas hymns.

Christmas Day is observed quietly. Business places and shops are closed, as they are also on the next day, the principal feature being the Christmas dinner — chicken, oranges, nuts, and pastries. Christmas is a season of prayer and quiet rejoicing, the children giving their saved pennies for the relief of the poor.

January 1 is the Day of Circumcision, a day of rejoicing. Now presents are exchanged. Children go from door to door while the wives remain at home to serve the guests with Turkish coffee and sweetmeats. January 2 is the women's visiting day.

Among the many beliefs related to Epiphany Eve, January 6, the most universally accepted one relates that just at midnight every tree bends its trunk and inclines its branches in homage to the Christ-child.

In southern Syria the gentle camel of Jesus travels over the desert and brings presents to the children, supposedly the youngest camel of those which brought the Wise Men to the manger! Which makes it how old? In their childhood faith they leave bowls of water and bowls of wheat outside their door. In the morning the good children find gifts, the others a black mark on the wrist!

8. Christmas in the Far East
and the Antipodes

WHILE, on the whole, the Christmas festival is new to the countries and peoples of the Far East and the Antipodes and many of the customs current there were introduced by Christian missionaries from the West, it is amazing to see the spontaneity that manifests itself regarding certain details that make the observance in this area of the world take on its own unique form. Gifted leaders have produced not only new native music for the special season, but new significance has come to be attached to native customs, especially to festive decorations.

Australia

To understand Christmas in Australia we need to remember that there are three distinct groups of people on this smallest of the continents and that it comes in midsummer when scorching hot days and the summer vacation season are to be reckoned with.

First, there are the native blacks, mostly uncivilized and unchristianized and therefore without an interest in a serious celebration of Christmas. Then there are the bushmen, mostly of

English background. Finally, there are the English people of the cities and towns and also smaller groups of other European backgrounds.

Both the groups interested in the day have shifted Christmas celebrations to the outdoors. This is no climate for mufflers and yule logs. Generally Christmas carols portray white beaches, blue waters, spreading gum trees or sun-drenched plains, peculiarly Australian; but quite often they include snow-capped roofs, holly, white-bearded " Father Christmas," or the snows and soft candles of the countries on the other side of the world.

The widespread distribution of gifts has been deeply ingrained. They are ascribed interchangeably to Father Christmas and to Santa Claus. They are exchanged at the breakfast table, and then there follows a Christmas service at the church. A Christmas dinner of roast beef or of fowl is common. Usually the remainder of the day is spent at the beaches (Australia has a 12,000-mile coast line), with a substantial supper resembling our Fourth-of-July picnics.

Since the end of the year, climatically, is the ideal time for vacations, factories, mines, offices, schools, and institutions close, and their entire staffs " take to the road " as the budgets permit. Just to be home for Christmas, it may be. If some member of the family happens to be off in the hills shearing or herding sheep, he will do his best to join his family in this season.

For several days before Christmas, greens and flowers can be bought for decorating the homes. Two of these are the Christmas bush and the Christmas bell. The first grows abundantly and is a multiple of tiny flowers growing in soft, hazy clusters. The Christmas bell is a bell-shaped flower, fringed in yellow and with bright green leaves. The youngsters use, in addition, huge ferns and palm leaves for decorating and hang green foliage over the front door.

The second Christmas Day is a time for sports. The whole family drives to the entertainment centers, taking along a picnic lunch. It is a day of special joy for the children.

A unique Australian contribution to Christmas tradition is **Carols by Candlelight**, a development of the small bands of carol singers that tell of Good King Wenceslas in the snows of English streets on Christmas Eve. Australia's carol-singing — again conditioned by the agreeable climate — is done by hundreds of thousands of people who gather in the spacious parks of the big capital cities and raise their voices in the balmy air of an Australian summer night illuminated by candlelight and torch flare.

The Australian pattern for Christmas has, perhaps, not moved so far at all from the European; perhaps a benevolent climate has made it more of a national festival, a time for a healthful break in the summer, but it is, as ever, predominantly a joyous festival of the Christian church. Although the demands of commerce may accelerate the tempo and the carnival spirit may be well in evidence, Christmas Day itself retains its inherent sanctity and religious significance. Industry and commerce cease, lights burn late in churches, and in the quiet of the day the Australian, like Christians everywhere, remembers his blessings and his friends.

Ceylon

In Ceylon we have an illustration of the two extremes — pagan superstition and the Christian Christmas.

On Christmas Eve, in Kandy, Ceylon, a grotesque celebration is held. Lanterns, torches, and huge bonfires light up the dark night. Then the drums begin to beat; fireworks are displayed; and a strange devil dance is performed.

In contrast to this are the simple but beautiful Christmas carols sung by the young people of Christian mission groups. Christian worship services hallow both Christmas Eve and Christmas Day. As typical of a Christmas service on an Oriental mission field, we give extracts from a missionary's letter:

Before dawn, while our household is yet deep in sleep, we hear faintly the melody, " Hark! the Herald Angels Sing." The carolers wend their way along the road, and their voices fade away, and with lighted lanterns we make our way to the church. A stream of lantern lights is coming down the hill as church members from nearby homes are joining the procession to the Christmas sunrise service.

At last all are in the church. The interior is dark except for the lanterns that the worshipers carry, but the semidarkness lends sanctity to it all. Paper chains in green, red, yellow, and blue are suspended in interlocking festoons overhead. On the white walls are posted large elaborate characters meaning " Peace " and " Joy." In front and to the left stands the Tree of Life, as the native Christians call the Christmas tree. It has no candles (a precaution against fire), but it is decked out with paper flowers, colored paper chains, paper bells, and cotton snowflakes.

The service begins. The congregation sings " O Little Town of Bethlehem " and " Once in David's Royal City "; the Christmas story is read from the Scriptures; prayers are offered by various members of the congregation; then after more singing the program comes to an end, and we return to our homes for breakfast.

At ten o'clock the main service is held. The worshipers, now grown to a crowd, are eager to hear the program. There are musical numbers furnished by the Girls' School and the Boys' School. One or more of these selections may be in English, because the students like to try out their newly acquired language. There are recitations of Scripture and there are dialogues. Dramatizations are a prominent feature. I clearly remember how realistically one group of girls acted out the carrying of the Christmas message to the poor folks in the countryside. Next there are some talks on the meaning of Christmas, and finally the offering is lifted for the poor.

For the children the climax is reached when the gifts are distributed. The packages contain such things as tangerines, peanuts, pretty colored picture cards (sometimes used Christmas cards that some friend from the United States has sent for just such occasions), Chinese candy, and Western lead pencils.

After the benediction the congregation disbands. During the afternoon various church members pay visits to other members, bringing and sharing humble gifts, and enriching the day in Christian fellowship.   (*Furnished by Rev. Theophilus Hilgemann.*)

China (Old China)

Aside from uncertainties because of changes in the last decade or two, it is necessary for us to remember that out of China's

500,000,000 population, there are only about 3,000,000 Catholics and 1,000,000 Protestants on the Chinese mainland; and about 35,000 Catholics and 150,000 Protestants on the island province of Formosa (Taiwan to the Chinese), bastion of free China. The masses of the Chinese people observe their " Christmas " festivity at New Year's, now officially called the Spring Festival and occurring toward the end of January. It is at this time that the children receive new clothes, eat more luxurious meals, and welcome new toys and firecrackers. The most important occasion of New Year's Eve is the ancestral worship. Portraits and paintings of ancestors to the fourth and fifth generations are brought out and hung on the walls of the main room of the home.

Even though the Chinese New Year's celebration is far more common than the observance of Christmas, the people are very fond of the bright colors of the Christmas decorations and have adopted them from their friends, the missionaries. They like the red holly berries and the green leaves of the holly, the bright tinsel and mellow lights. To these decorations they have added their own attractive Chinese lanterns. On Christmas Day gifts are exchanged, but strict rules prevail. Silks, jewels, and other comparatively valuable gifts are exchanged only within the immediate families. Gifts of food or cut flowers are common for more distant relatives and friends. While Christmas has been celebrated in some sections of China for four hundred years, the vast majority of its hundreds of millions of people have never heard of Christ.

Among the avowed Christians and wherever the Christmas spirit has penetrated, Christmas is a day of happiness and excitement. The little children hang up their stockings and welcome their dolls like their Western cousins do. Santa Claus is known as *Lan Khoong* (Nice Old Father) or as *Dun Che Lao Ren* (Christmas Old Man).

In order to preserve for posterity and make conveniently available glimpses of Christmas observances among first-generation Christians in the Orient, we share with our readers several more letters from friends who rendered devoted service in these areas. First we quote from one from Karl Beck, a missionary in China in the 1930's:

Last Christmas season the Cosmopolitan Club at State College, Pennsylvania, held a very interesting meeting at which a representative from every country whose natives were present was requested to tell of the Christmas customs of his own country. The Chinese student who responded said that the Chinese people do not have Christmas, and so have no Christmas customs; then he told at length about the New Year's customs of his people.

The Christian people, throughout China, however, do observe Christmas. And in some communities where the church exerts a large influence, it is not only the church members who observe the holiday, but even a number of the business people and government officials exchange Christmas greetings and decorate their homes in honor of the day. Some churches consider Easter to be the most important and significant day of the church year. But Christmas has a large place, particularly in the life of the children.

While there is some exchanging of Christmas presents among Chinese Christians, the general token of mutual remembrance is the post-card greeting. Within one classis or synod, for instance, the congregations, through their consistories, exchange greetings. Friends, and especially colleagues in Christian work, remember each other in this way. One or two city post offices gave notice that they would not receive Christmas greetings for transmittance. This was because there was no provision in the management of the Chinese postal service to increase employees to handle the extra mail. That had to do not only with the office staff but also with runners, by whom mail is still carried through large parts of the country.

In one of our congregations, it has long been a custom for the members of the church to have a Christmas meal together. While this was a simple meal, still there were some of the families who could not afford to join in. This gave opportunity for those who were able to do so, to evidence the spirit of the day by being hosts, in a sense, to their less prosperous fellow Christians.

In a mission boys' school, such as Huping, Christmas is thought of and prepared for by the students in the following ways:

The social-service committee of the Y.M.C.A. announces that, as usual, the poor of the neighborhood are to be remembered at this season. Students and teachers, as well as farmer members of the congregation, are asked to prepare such contribution as they can make in food, clothing, and money. These are collected prior to Christmas Day, much in the spirit of a " White Gifts for the King " project. On Christmas Day, or before or after that — depending on when the first severe cold spell of the winter arrives — the supplies are taken to the homes of the needy villagers. Half of the Christmas Day Freewill Offering is usually added to this Y.M.C.A. local relief fund. The other half of the offering is sent to some congregation at a distance — perhaps in another province — that is known to be suffering from famine, or plague, or other affliction.

The day before Christmas is usually free from classes. Part of the student body is feverishly busy preparing for the Christmas dramatics. The others are organized into groups to decorate the various meeting places where the services and entertainments will be held. And, of course, there are the final practices for the Christmas service itself, which is very largely a service of song. The program may begin with a Christmas Eve lantern parade. The Order for Christmas Day will be about as follows:

Carol-singing, before dawn.

Candlelight service in the chapel as dawn breaks.

Christmas service at ten o'clock.

Afternoon dramatization, beginning at two o'clock.

Reception, with tea and cakes, to the families of the community, in connection with the dramatization.

Group fellowship meetings (for social fellowship or for devotions, according to the disposition of each group) held during the evening.

It is probable that a group of students, with some Christian leader, will go for the Christmas vacation to some island or mountain temple for retreat and Bible study.

Christmas Day, because it is the day that honors the memory of the birth of Jesus, is respected by all who know about Jesus. His way of life and his teachings are respected even by people who do not join the church.

Now we bring our readers a letter that reflects the transition from Old China to New China, sent us by Rev. Robert Bausum of Mt. Vernon, Kentucky.

Our field, as you probably know, is China. Until the closing of the mainland by the communists, we were in South-Central China, at a city called Kweilin, some 200 miles inland from Canton. After the closing of the mainland we have been assigned to the mission force on Formosa — Taiwan to the Chinese.

It must be remembered that there were NO CHRISTMAS CUS-TOMS at all until the missionaries brought the message of Christ to the Chinese. Therefore, naturally, and inevitably, most of the customs now observed by the people there are:

1. limited to the actual Christian constituency; and

2. shaped largely by the customs prevailing in the homeland of the missionary — often altered to fit convictions held by those missionaries; for example, some missionaries have convictions about the use or nonuse of Christmas trees. Naturally they would lead their converts to follow those convictions. I have even seen a Santa Claus in China, with all the trimmings!

Basically, however, the Chinese consider the occasion one of worship and respond more readily to the religious significance of the occasion. We always had a church service on Christmas Day, and it was about the biggest service of the year. Sometimes we distributed oranges or bags of candy to the children; but this became impossible to control in an orderly fashion and was discontinued. They often put on a play, following the Scripture very closely; and the hymns they sing are, of course, mostly translations of our familiar hymns.

The Chinese are much less likely to have a feast on Christmas Day. Since their traditional New Year's Day follows so soon, they save the big feast for that day.

Christmas cards are beginning to be plentiful and somewhat commercialized. Many follow traditional " Western " style, but many are exquisite samples of Chinese art adapted to the occasion. Often the figures of " The Holy Family " appear — with Chinese features!

General exchange of presents has not reached anything like the mass proportions it has with us. Indeed, it hardly prevails unless as a concession to the " Foreigner " and his customs.

Formosa

Finally, we furnish a letter that brings us up to date since it describes Christmas in Formosa in 1955, indicating, among other things, the large place that music of an advanced type occupies among our friends in the Orient. The report is by Mrs. J. N. Montgomery and appeared in the *Presbyterian Survey*, December, 1956:

Christmas in Formosa is a musical one. Some of the early missionaries — both English in the south and Canadians in the north — were musicians who helped to develop a musical church. Handel's *The Messiah*, as well as other cantatas and oratorios, is beloved and sung by several choirs each year.

Some performances are musically worthy; all are in a worshipful spirit that makes them blessed experiences. All the Christmas music loved around the world is used. Several distinctive Chinese hymns are favorites.

Usually there is an illustrated program mimeographed in color, giving the hymns for congregational singing written in full.

Different choirs and groups go caroling in the midnight hours. Some use chartered buses to cover longer distances. Hospitals and other institutions are visited. Christmas is a time for ministering to the needy.

In addition to music, Scripture recitation and tableaux in costume are much used — especially having little children do them. " Because it is an expression of joy and gladness," one student answered my query.

Elaborate dramatizations have been attempted with remarkable success by some groups, bringing enthusiastic enjoyment to the audiences. *The Other Wise Man, Quo Vadis?* and *Les Misérables* have all been used for Christmas plays.

The Nativity scenes and flowers decorate private homes and public places. The poinsettia, " the Christmas flower," grows luxuriantly in Formosa and blooms from November to March, decorating many streets and lanes as its crimson flowers tower above high walls. Pots of them are used freely inside and out at Christmas time. Cedars and pines constitute Christmas trees.

Big scenes with stars, angels, shepherds, and Wise Men decorate church walls. Sometimes Santas, sleighs, and reindeer have a prominence startling to some of us. Streamers and paper chains are augmented by big red and gold Chinese ideographs that are both beautiful and meaningful.

Gifts include candy made of rice flour and sugar, decorated with Christmas symbols — a steamed delicacy something like a solid marshmallow — good!

One church group from the mainland has had, for five years, a " Together Meal " at Christmas time. They engage space in a restaurant, visit together around big tables, have happy fellowship and a good meal, with some singing and talks.

This has been a great help to family feeling for many uprooted from old homes. Usually each one pays for his own meal, but it gives an opportunity to invite guests and to have some who do not have the means to pay their way.

Greeting cards are increasingly used, some very elaborate and beautiful. Christians want Christian messages. Many are displayed in shops in bigger cities. Many people are using them as a social device. Some families and friends are beginning to exchange gifts, though New Year's, through long custom, is still the gift time for most people in the lunar year.

In Formosa generally, Sunday is observed as a different day. Banks and big businesses close, and there is no regular schoolwork. Since there is no Christmas holiday, a Sunday Christmas is a boon. Christian schools give the one day, but Christmas activities fill the weekends nearest Christmas, and New Year's is a big day too, a general holiday.

Christmas is then a Christian festival in Formosa, and the churches make it a time of joyful witness.

Japan

The Japanese do not have any really popular native Christmas songs as yet, but every Japanese Christian, in fact almost every educated Japanese, knows the Japanese translation of " Joy to the World," " Holy Night," and similar international hymns.

The Christmas festival has become a Japanese festival on the secular side. In this small, heavily populated country, though there are but 500,000 Christians of the 91,000,000 population, the radio reaches millions conveniently. Huge Christmas trees adorn the department stores, and tiny ones are placed in the windows of smaller shops. Paper holly and bells and festoons in red and green are seen everywhere, and even Christmas " sales " are becoming common. Practically every Japanese knows the word " Christmas " and associates it with gift-giving and a good time generally. In fact, an editorial in a Japanese daily newspaper complained bitterly that Christmas was driving out the old national festival of New Year's.

The more definitely religious observance can be illustrated by observing Sendai, a typical provincial capital. There Christian mission work has been going on for some seventy-five years, resulting in the establishing of large Christian churches. A Christmas concert in recent years, though it included some secular songs, was predominantly sacred. On Christmas Eve, Christmas hymns and carols are sent by radio all over the Empire.

Sunday school celebrations are similar to those in America, with many Japanese touches added, of course. Pageant-plays of the Christmas story, with the characters largely in Japanese dress, are popular. The dramas are presented so realistically that you can imagine yourself back on Bethlehem's plains 2,000 years ago. Each Christian group has a service of Bible selections, prayers, and hymns and quite generally a tea party, or at least a " cake party," since a bag or box of Japanese cakes goes to each person in attendance. Caroling begins as early as three and four o'clock in the morning. Red Japanese lanterns produce a picturesque sight.

In country villages at Sunday school services the children sit on the matted floor in front, and behind them the crowd packs the limited quarters to capacity, most of them wearing the padded winter kimono. Eagerly they listen to the Christmas story vividly told.

Christmas for missionaries in Japan is a wonderful time, generally lasting a month or more. Several missionaries have begun the custom of having a Christmas tree and a service and entertainment in their home for the children living in the same block. With a number of Japanese Christians adopting this plan, the Christmas message will cheer the hearts of an ever-increasing number.

In November, groups meet weekly, cutting the pictures from used Christmas cards with a religious message and pasting them carefully on the front of printed Christmas tracts. Although most of the women are not yet Christians themselves, they work on the project with enthusiasm and devotion.

We note then that Christmas is meaningful among Japanese Christians and also beyond their number. It cannot be as much a family day as in our country, since there are comparatively few families in which every member is a Christian, though that number is increasing. Neither are turkey and plum pudding nearly so common. But it is a day on which a high proportion of the Christians try to do something for others, especially for the sick in the hospitals. Although most of the hospitals are unattractive, without suitable rooms for holding meetings, Christian young people decorate whatever space is allowed with a small tree and a " back " (a piece of black cloth upon which are fastened stars, shepherds, and Wise Men cut from cardboard).

The very best students are chosen from the Sunday school to sing Christmas carols for the patients, to recite Bible passages, and to put on a short drama or Bible pantomime. And then, of course, there is always a treat of cakes or candies for the Bible-class patients, and Christmas tracts for everyone in the hospital — from the superintendent and the chief surgeon to the scrub woman.

The following testimony of a college girl is characteristic of many: " I experienced my first Christmas at Kobe College (December, 1954); it was different from any kind I had ever had before. Before last Christmas, I experienced Christmas only as enjoying myself, and I held parties with my friends and feasted. Now I take a delight in serving others. At first I knitted socks for orphans and helped with a Christmas program of the Sunday school. When I went back to my home, I had no money left for gifts. I had experienced the true Christmas spirit and am looking forward to such a Christmas again this year."

Even more touching and far-reaching are these words from a freshman: " At Christmas in 1954 I enjoyed many significant experiences. The most valuable and memorable thing is my baptism. I was baptized at Hikone Church, December 19, 1954. This experience is my great progression, I think. My father, mother, and many friends attended this ceremony and blessed me with strong handshaking. I couldn't find words for my response. I was filled with happiness and thanksgiving. My sister was glad for my experience and cried through the ceremony. She played the organ and at my request played *Passacaglia* by Bach. I like this music, and it will resound in my life. Now I look in my mind to our God, and I am very happy."

Christmas for Christians in Japan means Christ coming again into their hearts with new power. It means Christ coming for the first time into hearts that have never known him before. Thus it is truly a " Meri Kurisumasu! "

Korea

In Korea, Christmas celebrations are held in various places. In the Christian schools the student bodies usually present some drama in addition to the more formal service. In the churches the Sunday schools and young people's organizations often have their programs earlier, since Christmas Day is occupied by the whole church organization with its special services.

The early-morning caroling is a very happy and impressive part of the program on Christmas Day. On Christmas Eve, Sunday school children, young people, and some of the church officers gather together in the church and pass the night, sleepless, dividing into groups. At two o'clock the next morning they start toward the different sections of the parish, singing hymns in front of every parishioner's house. Inside the door the family members wake up and come out to the door to express their thanks. Some families invite them into the house and entertain them with a simple provision. By the time all have been thus favored, the beautiful day is dawning.

The Christmas service of the whole congregation is usually held at half past ten or eleven o'clock in the morning. The church auditorium and the gates are beautifully decorated. In the program of the service many special features are introduced, such as singing by the church choir and Sunday school children, addresses by the children and by a special speaker. The offering is generally one of money, though many people bring packages of rice and clothes to be given to the poor.

To give us a realistic glimpse, through the description and the implications, we shall let Joseph B. Hopper, missionary in Chunju, Korea, tell us about " Christmas for 822 Korean Orphans in 1955."

A thousand little hearts to fill with Christmas joy! A thousand little tummies to fill with hot, steaming rice, beef stew, and *kimchi* (most famous of Korean appetizers)! This was the reason for the Christmas party for children at four Chunju orphanages and one refugee camp in the vicinity. A dozen or more volunteer workers, inspired and led by Mrs. W. A. Linton, joined a group of teachers from our Girls' School in preparing the celebration.

Weeks in advance great jars of *kimchi* were prepared, a cow was butchered, five hundred pounds of rice were cooked. Forty students from the mission Bible schools, who serve as Sunday school teachers in these orphanages, worked out an elaborate program for the morning. Lighted Christmas trees decorated the boys' gymnasium, and two large classrooms were converted into dining rooms complete with small tables and benches.

The day dawned crisp and cold, but this meant nothing to the truckloads of children who drove into town singing gaily. In six-ton trucks furnished by the Korean Civil Assistance Command, they arrived at the gymnasium and streamed inside to sit in rows on the floor. Most wore clothes made by a group of widows whose husbands had been killed by the communists. These women, working with materials supplied by the Korean Civil Assistance Command, have produced literally thousands of garments for the orphanages of the province.

For two hours the children entertained themselves. Music, recitations, and pageants were produced by children from the Sunday schools of these institutions. The most elaborate pageant presented the whole Christmas story acted by the big boys of one orphanage. These children, who rarely see things of beauty or enjoy entertainment of any kind, stared starry-eyed at the Christmas tree lights, the stage decorations, and the costumed characters.

But the height of the occasion was the feast. A few little spoons found their way to hungry mouths before the blessing was said, but when that was over it was a sight to behold.

Most of these children get enough to eat regularly, but it is usually a rather monotonous grain mush. Here was steaming white rice, and what more can a Korean want? Grubby hands lifted great chunks of *kimchi* and literally dropped them into wide-open mouths. When chopsticks and spoons failed to work fast enough, bowls of beef stew were raised to the lips.

Again and again attendants filled the bowls until no one could eat a bite more.

As the children filed out, they were handed bags of fruit and candy. In addition, each received an especially marked pencil and notebook given by the students of the Boys' and Girls' Schools as their Christmas offering.

By actual count 822 children were fed that day, and the remaining food was taken to the orphanages for those too small to come to the party.

As the trucks moved off loaded with singing children, we could thank God for the opportunity of bringing this Christmas joy to so many who have tasted such bitterness, and of telling them the story of Him who came to seek and to save that which was lost.

Those at home can rejoice that they had a part in this joy through their contributions to the relief budget of the Department of Overseas Relief, which made this happy occasion possible.

> All glory be to God on high,
> And to the earth be peace:
> Good will henceforth, from heaven to men,
> Begin and never cease!
> — *Nahum Tate*

New Guinea

" A Christmas Play and Party " in a New Guinea Hospital reported in the *Lutheran Women's Missionary Outlook*, December, 1956, gives us an unforgettable picture of the observance of the season in that distant land.

It was December 23, in New Guinea. A Christmas play and party had been planned for the Buangi hospital. Some of the student doctors and their families had worked on the play for a long time to get it ready. The little children took the parts of the angels, sheep, and cattle; but the older children took the parts of Mary, Joseph, the shepherds, and the Wise Men. Metti and Anui, student doctors, read the story while the pantomime was acted by the little folk. Since they had copied their costumes directly from Bible pictures, everything was probably much the way it had been many years before in Bethlehem, except that the baby Jesus really belonged to Sukie, and he was just as black as he could be! Nobody minded that, though, for they all knew that God had sent Jesus to them just as much as he had sent him to the white men, and they were remembering once again the wonderful gift that had come at Christmastide.

Everything went smoothly. The angel spoke to Mary, the angel choir sang, the sheep and cattle moved at the right moments and were properly restless with the beautiful baby in their midst. When the shepherds arrived, little Yalesu, who played the baby Jesus, started to cry. He really didn't know any better. He was the son of one of the student doctors and just nine days old. Everything stopped. The readers were quiet, the actors wondered what to do, and even the audience was horrified at this break in the lovely story.

In a moment, the baby's father picked him out of the manger and handed him to his mother in the audience; then he borrowed another baby, for there were many, and settled it in the manger; and the play went on. Little Koy never knew the difference, and lay there happily sucking his thumb until the Wise Men departed and his real mother came to claim him.

As the stage was cleared off, everyone sang the New Guinea version of Christmas carols, which sounded peculiar in our ears, but meant just as much peace and good will to them as do ours to us. Now was the time everyone likes best the world over — time for presents. Women in America had made dresses and loin cloths, with warm woolen jackets for the cool nights, and brightly colored panties for the children. Each student doctor received gifts for himself and his family. Since they earn less than fifty dollars a year, perhaps you can guess how happy they were to have new things.

One church back in Ohio had sent dolls to Mrs. Madden, and

each child received one. Their little faces lit up like candles, beaming with radiance. How much happiness had a little time, effort, and love from those far away brought these simple people!

Of course, no party is complete without refreshments. Soon sandwiches and tea were served to everyone. Banana and pineapple made a wonderful dessert, and everyone, natives and missionaries alike, felt they had truly celebrated the Christ-child's birthday. Parents and children walked happily home, calling " Bubiang, . . . thank you," with every heart singing carols of joy that Jesus had come to set men free from fear, saving their souls for eternity.

New Zealand

In New Zealand, Christmas Day itself is observed in much the same way as it is in the United States and in Europe. There are some concessions to the reversed seasons, however, for Christmas " down under " comes in midsummer. On the New Zealand Christmas dinner menu, for instance, plum pudding is almost invariably flanked by fruit salad, ice cream, and fresh summer fruits such as strawberries and raspberries.

In New Zealand, as in the rest of Christendom, Christmas is pre-eminently the season for reaffirming good will and friendship for the gathering and reunion of friends and families. For several weeks before December 25, New Zealanders crowd the shops and department stores looking for presents for their families and close friends, and for greeting cards for a wider circle of acquaintances. Every big store has a professional Santa Claus, white-bearded, red-mantled, black-booted, perspiringly presiding over a " Magic Cave " or a " Toyland," and solemnly noting the Christmas Eve requirements of hundreds of excited children.

Noncommercial organizations also arrange Christmas parties for children, particularly for the orphans, the sick, and the crippled. Such organizations, in town and country, are the Rotary Clubs, the war veterans' societies — such as the Returned Services (or Veterans) Association, the Commercial Travelers Association, and many others. The summer weather allows many of these children's parties to be held outdoors, the main ingredients being candies, ice cream, toy gifts — often from a Christmas tree — fancy dress, races, games, and competitions.

Christmas Eve is much the same in New Zealand as it is in this country. A last feverish flurry of shopping is made possible by a special late night in the stores, and then families and friends may gather for a Christmas Eve party at home. There are few homes in which children do not carefully hang up their stockings for Santa Claus to fill with toys and candies. There are midnight services at the churches for those who observe the original significance of Christmas, and special broadcasts of Christmas programs on the radio network. Carol-singing has also been inherited from the Old World, and in some towns on Christmas Eve, " Carols by Candlelight " are held in suitable settings outdoors.

Christmas Day is often ushered in by carol-singing, as in countries of the northern hemisphere. Perhaps the most popular and most regular carolers are those of the Salvation Army group, whose melodious rendering of the well-loved old Christmas hymns wakens many New Zealanders on the morning of the Nativity celebration.

New Zealanders spend their Christmas Day in much the same way as do Christians elsewhere, with the friendly greetings, the gifts — and especially the toys for the children — and the sumptuous family dinner. Christmas dinner in New Zealand usually includes poultry of some sort — turkey, chicken, duck, or goose — meat joints such as lamb, pork, beef, or mutton, the new season's peas, potatoes, and other vegetables, mince pies, plum pudding, and the rest of traditional fare inherited from New Zealand's British ancestry. But in most homes, dishes more suitable to summer weather are added to the menu, and in many cases replace it. There are salads, cold poultry, fresh fruit, and cold sweet dishes.

In the northern hemisphere Christmas, coming in midwinter, is a comparatively brief break in the year. Where Christmas comes in summer, however, as in New Zealand, Australia, parts of Africa, and other countries with a warm December, it is vacation time, and it makes a logical interval between the end of one year and the beginning of the next. Particularly in recent years, New Zealanders have become great travelers within their own country. Theirs is a country well known for its rich and varied scenic attractions, which are spread through the length and breadth of the land. In both the North and the South Islands there are beautiful rivers, lakes, and mountains, unparalleled thermal wonders, pleasant bathing beaches, and outstanding scenery of all types. As a result, no matter where a person lives in New Zealand, there is always something worth-while for him to see in another part of the country.

In the proportion of automobiles to population, New Zealand is second only to the United States, and throughout the summer the roads carry a tremendous traffic of motorists on vacation — many with tents or trailers, known in New Zealand as caravans. The temperate climate makes camping enjoyable, and the well-organized automobile associations maintain well-equipped camping sites or trailer parks at the most popular resorts.

Throughout the summer the ranks of tourists from other countries are swelled too by thousands of New Zealanders traveling by train, ship, and plane — as well as on bicycles and on foot — to see more of their own country. From Christmas Day, through New Year's Day, and well into January and February, New Zealand is a nation on holiday. Most people take their two to three weeks' vacation at some time during this period, though essential industries and services — particularly transport — " stagger " their holiday periods to interfere as little as possible with public needs.

Schools go into recess for six or seven weeks, starting about a week before Christmas Day, and universities complete their examinations by about the first week in December, resuming lectures in the first week of the following March. Shops, factories, and businesses close down at least for Christmas Day and the two following days, and then for New Year's Day and January 2; but many firms and professional men take their long vacation at this time, closing down altogether for two to three weeks, from Christmas Day onward.

Not only do individuals and families take advantage of New Zealand's summertime Christmas, for many organizations — academic, professional, sporting, business, religious, and cultural — arrange annual conventions, summer schools, tramping parties, music or drama festivals, athletic meetings, at this time, usually at tourist or health resorts.

In New Zealand, the Christmas–New Year period — the "weekend" of the year — occurs at the logical time for rest and relaxation. The feast is revered for its message of Christianity, but it brings in its train days of sunshine and recreation, in which the people may renew their strength for the coming year.

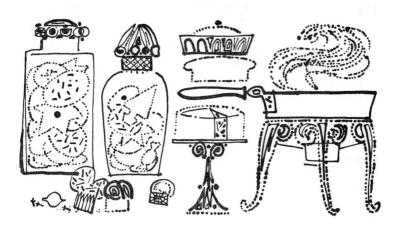

9. Recipes from Around the World

WHEREVER there are festivities, food always plays a significant role. So it is not surprising that certain foods have come to be associated with the observance of Christmas. Over against feasting and carousing, there is a legitimate place for the Christmas turkey with all the trimmings, enjoyed in the United States not merely by the prosperous, nor only by the middle class, but provided for the poorest, freely and bountifully, by groups like the Salvation Army and numerous welfare agencies.

Quite literally and quite universally the advice that Poor Robin gave in his *Almanack* for 1700 is heeded:

> Now that the time has come wherein
> Our Saviour Christ was born,
> The larder's full of beef and pork,
> The granary's full of corn.
> As God hath plenty to thee sent,
> Take comfort of thy labors,
> And let it never thee repent
> To feed thy needy neighbors.

While there is no need of repeating at length the numerous excellent recipes available in cookbooks and in daily newspapers

153

and periodicals, our readers will no doubt appreciate a " handy reference list " of selected Christmas foods that can easily be prepared. Inclusion of these delicious dishes should also help foster appreciation for the peoples of other lands and backgrounds.

Armenia (Old Armenia)

In Armenia all the villages fast one week before Christmas by eating no animal food and no food at all on the last day. On Christmas Eve, *Pilav*, a rice or wheat food, is eaten. After the church service, fried fish, lettuce, and spinach constitute the menu, since it is believed that spinach was the food that Mary ate on the eve of Christ's birth.

BOULGEUR PILAV

1 small onion	¾ cup lamb
1 cup rice or cracked wheat (can be cracked in a coffee mill)	2 tsp. salt
	3 tbsp. melted butter
	¼ tsp. pepper
3 cups water	

Cut meat into cubes, and put into a saucepan with water and salt. Let boil until meat is nearly done. Then add rice or cracked wheat and cook 30 minutes, not allowing the stock to reduce to less than 2½ cups. Brown finely chopped onion in butter and pour over the meat. Set aside for 15 minutes to settle.

Colombia

BUNUELOS (*Christmas Dessert*)

2½ oz. butter	Grated rind of 1 lemon
⅔ cup sugar	1 cup water
3 eggs, well beaten	Flour

Mix butter, sugar, and lemon rind together well. Add eggs, water, and enough flour to make a soft dough. Spread out the dough on a kneading board and cut off small pieces.

Drop in deep fat which must not be too hot. When brown, remove and drain on paper. Serve sprinkled with powdered sugar and cinnamon, or with sirup or honey.

Czechoslovakia

KOLAGE (*Christmas Rounds*)

1 cup butter	2 quarts bread flour
1 cup sugar	1 cake yeast
3 egg yolks	1 quart milk

To 1 cup of the milk which is heated until lukewarm, add 1 tsp. of the sugar, yeast, and a little flour to make a very thin batter. Set aside in a warm place to rise. Cream butter, add remaining sugar and the egg yolks. Beat. Add the yeast mixture, the flour, and as much more of the milk (lukewarm) as is necessary for a dough of medium thickness. Beat well and place in warm place to rise. When light, take some of the dough and put on floured board, cut in small pieces, shape in small balls, and place on buttered pan about 4 inches apart. Press each ball in the center to make a hollow and fill either with cottage cheese filling, poppyseed, or prune filling. Let rise again and bake in a moderate oven. When done, brush over with melted butter and sprinkle with powdered sugar.

PRUNE FILLING

1 lb. prunes	1 tbsp. lemon juice
1 cup sugar	Cinnamon to taste

Boil prunes, stone, and put through chopper. Mix well with sugar, lemon juice, and cinnamon.

Denmark

DANISH JULEKAKE

2 cups milk	1 tsp. cardamon seeds, ground
1 cake yeast	1 tsp. salt
½ lb. raisins	1 egg
⅓ lb. butter	½ cup sugar
½ lb. citron, or less	Flour, to make soft dough

Mix the milk, yeast cake, salt, sugar, butter, egg, and flour as you would for ordinary bread. Let rise and knead well on bread board. Add cardamon seed, citron, and raisins. Let rise again. Form into two loaves. Let rise in pans and brush over with milk or butter. Bake about ½ hour.

England

Of the many tasty dishes served in English homes at Christmas, we furnish recipes here for two.

ENGLISH CHRISTMAS BREAD

¼ cup raisins	¼ tsp. nutmeg
¼ cup citron	½ tsp. allspice
1 package yeast	½ tsp. caraway seed
¼ cup warm water	½ cup boiling water
¼ cup sugar	⅓ cup nonfat milk solids
¼ cup butter or margarine	3 cups sifted all-purpose flour,
1 tsp. salt	approximately

Chop raisins and citron. Soften yeast in warm water. Add boiling water to sugar, butter, salt, and spices and cool to lukewarm. Combine nonfat milk solids and 1 cup flour and add to the cooled mixture. Add softened yeast and beat until smooth. Blend in half the remaining flour and fruits and add remaining flour gradually to make a soft dough. Turn dough out on a lightly floured pastry cloth and knead until smooth. Place dough in a greased bowl and turn once to bring greased side up. Cover and let rise in a warm place until double in bulk (1½–2 hours). Turn dough out on a pastry cloth, knead, and shape into 2 loaves. Place in greased pans 6 x 3½ x 2¼ inches. Let rise until double in bulk (about 1½ hours). Bake in a slow oven (325° F.) for 1 hour. Makes two small loaves.

YORKSHIRE SALAD

3 tbsp. molasses	2 heads lettuce, shredded
6 tbsp. vinegar	3 scallions (green onions)
½ tsp. black pepper	sliced fine

Combine the molasses, vinegar, and pepper in a bowl and mix well. Combine the lettuce and scallions and mix well. Pour the dressing over it. Toss until the lettuce is well coated with the dressing. Serve cold but not ice cold.

France

PETITS GATEAUX TAILLES

1 cup soft butter or margarine	Red food coloring
Sugar	½ tsp. almond flavoring
2½ cups sifted flour	Yellow food coloring
⅛ tsp. salt	Finely chopped nuts
1 tsp. rose water	

Can be frozen. Mix butter, 1 cup sugar, flour, and salt thoroughly. Divide dough; flavor half with rose water, and tint a delicate pink. Flavor other half with almond, and tint pale yellow. Shape each half into a roll 2 inches in diameter. Chill until firm. Cut in ⅛-inch slices, put on cooky sheets, and sprinkle centers with sugar and nuts. Bake in hot oven, 400° F., about 8 minutes. Makes about 6 dozen.

Germany

German households are said to begin their Christmas baking a whole month before Christmas. The following four recipes will always be of interest.

GERMAN CHRISTMAS COOKIES

1 quart sirup	1 pint lard and butter, mixed
1 cup sugar	

Warm all together a little, then add:

1 tbsp. cloves	1 tsp. allspice
1 tbsp. salt	1 tsp. ginger
1 tbsp. cinnamon	2 eggs
1 tsp. nutmeg	½ cup sour milk
1 tbsp. soda dissolved in a little hot water	1 oz. anise seed
	¼ lb. citron, cut fine
	Flour to make very stiff

It is best to leave the dough a week or two in a cold room, but it is quite tasty also when baked the next morning after mixing. It approaches the flavor of Pfeffernuesse and is doubly good when iced with powdered sugar only or when a little chocolate is added for extra flavor.

This recipe produces 10 to 15 dozen good-sized cookies. Smaller families may prefer to use one half the recipe, or share the whole amount with friends.

CHRISTMAS LEBKUCHEN

2 eggs (whole)	1½ lb. flour
4 egg yolks	½ oz. cinnamon
1 lb. sugar	1 tsp. ground cloves
⅓ lb. butter	½ tsp. nutmeg
½ lb. almonds	2½ tsp. baking powder
8 oz. citron, sliced thin	1 tsp. grated lemon rind

Melt butter over slow heat. Stir into it the sugar, spices, chopped almonds, and eggs (well beaten). Add flour slowly, the baking powder having previously been mixed well with the flour. Roll out the dough thin and cut into the shapes desired. Place half of one almond in the center of each cooky and brush top of each cooky with the white of egg. Bake in moderate oven (350 degrees) until brown.

PFEFFERNUESSE (*Pepper nuts or gingerbread nuts*)

1 lb. sugar	1 tsp. each, cinnamon, cloves,
1 lb. flour	and nutmeg
¼ lb. citron	Grated rind of 1 lemon
¼ lb. almonds	½ tsp. hartshorn crystals
4 eggs	(available at drugstores)

Beat together the eggs and sugar until light. Sift together the dry ingredients and add the hartshorn crystals which have been crushed well. Let dough stand overnight. Next day form balls, size of large walnut. Make a thin mixture of powdered sugar and milk and brush it on the cookies. Flatten them slightly, bake at 300 degrees until brown, possibly 20 minutes.

SPRINGERLE (*Hard cookies, anise flavor*)

4½ cups flour	1 lb. powdered sugar
1 tsp. baking powder	1 tbsp. grated lemon rind
4 eggs	Anise seed — ground or whole

Sift the flour and baking powder together. Beat the eggs until light and lemon colored; add sugar and beat again. Add lemon rind, then the flour mixture. Mix well, then chill about an hour, or until firm enough to handle easily. Then, on a lightly floured cloth-covered board, roll to ½-inch thickness. Traditionally, you must have a rolling pin with springerle designs: actually, you can cut the dough into small shapes of any kind. Place on a cooky sheet, ½ inch apart. Leave exposed to air overnight, first sprinkling with anise seed. Then bake at 350 degrees about 30 minutes.

Greece

TEA BISCUIT

1 cup sugar	1 tsp. nutmeg
1 cup butter	1 tsp. cinnamon
3 eggs	½ tsp. soda
1 cup raisins	2 cups milk
2 lbs. flour	

Put sugar and butter in saucepan and cream for 5 minutes. Add 3 eggs and mix well. Add cup of raisins, nutmeg, cinnamon, soda, milk, and flour. Mix well and toss on lightly floured board and roll out very thin. Cut as desired. Put on greased baking sheet and bake in a moderate oven 12 to 15 minutes.

Hawaii

Elaborate dinners are commonly served in Hawaii, many of which include the following:

HAWAIIAN CHICKEN CURRY (*A holiday favorite*)

Make a large dish of creamed stewed chicken flavored with curry. Serve each guest boiled rice, then chicken. Pass a relish dish filled with the following: minced egg yolk, minced green and red peppers, dried fish, ground peanuts, chutney, sliced lemon. With this dish is served alligator pear and sliced tomato salad, and pineapple Bavarian cream for dessert.

Hungary

CHRISTMAS SEED COOKIES

2½ cups sifted cake flour	1 cup soft butter
½ tsp. baking powder	2 egg yolks
⅛ tsp. salt	1 tsp. vanilla
1 cup sugar	Seed such as caraway, sesame, anise

Sift dry ingredients; cut in butter. Add egg yolks and vanilla; blend. Chill several hours. Roll to ⅛-inch thickness on floured board, and cut in fancy shapes. Put on cooky sheets, and sprinkle with seed. Bake in hot oven, 400° F., about 8 minutes. Makes about 8 dozen small cookies.

Ireland

Ireland's cookery consists largely of plain and wholesome food — herring, trout, beef, lamb, poultry, game, potatoes, and other common vegetables. Among their Christmas delicacies are Soda Scones.

SODA SCONES

3 cups flour	1 tsp. salt
1 tsp. cream of tartar	1 tsp. baking soda
1 cup buttermilk	

Stir together the dry ingredients and mix lightly with the hands. Make a hollow in the center and add enough buttermilk to make a soft dough. Turn onto a floured board and knead quickly and lightly until the dough is free from cracks. Roll out the required thickness and cut in scones. Place on a greased and floured tin and bake in a hot oven (400 degrees) until thoroughly baked — about 15 minutes.

Italy
ITALIAN CHRISTMAS BREAD

2 packages yeast
½ cup warm water
¼ cup sugar
¾ tsp. salt
⅓ cup butter or margarine, melted
¼ cup water
⅓ cup nonfat milk solids

3¾ cups sifted all-purpose flour (approximately)
2 eggs
¾ tsp. vanilla
¼ cup white raisins
¼ cup almonds, chopped
2 tbsp. candied pineapple
¼ cup candied lemon peel

Soften yeast in warm water. Combine sugar, salt, butter, and remaining water. Combine nonfat milk solids and 1 cup flour. Remove a tablespoon of white from the eggs and reserve for glaze. Add remainder of eggs, vanilla, and softened yeast. Beat until smooth. Add 1 cup flour with fruit and nuts. Blend and add remaining flour gradually to form a soft dough. Turn out on a lightly floured pastry cloth and knead until smooth. Place in a greased bowl, turning once to bring greased side up. Cover and let rise in a warm place until double in bulk (1 hour and 20 minutes). Turn out on a pastry cloth and knead. Shape into a round loaf and place in a greased 8- or 9-inch round cake pan. Brush with egg white, cover, and let rise until double in bulk (40 minutes). Brush with egg white and bake in a slow oven (325° F.) for 55 to 60 minutes. Cover with foil after 15 minutes of baking to prevent overbrowning. Makes one round loaf.

Mexico
HOLIDAY SPICY ORANGE THINS

1 cup soft butter or margarine
1½ cups sugar
Grated rind 1 orange
1 egg
4 cups sifted flour

¾ tsp. salt
1 tsp. cinnamon
½ tsp. crushed cardamon seed
½ cup nuts ground fine
¼ cup orange juice

Cream butter; add sugar, orange rind, and egg; beat till light. Add remaining ingredients and mix well. Roll very thin, cut with floured cutters. Bake in 425° F. oven, 6 to 8 minutes. Makes 10 dozen.

Norway

SAND KAGER (A *holiday favorite*)

2 cups butter
2 cups sugar

1 cup finely chopped almonds
4 cups flour

Cream butter and sugar and work in flour and almonds with the hands until well mixed. Press into tins and bake until a delicate brown.

LINGONBERRY MOUSSE

1 cup farina
¼ tsp. salt
Whipping cream

1½ cups water
1 fourteen-oz. jar lingonberry
jam

Add farina slowly to boiling salted water, stirring constantly. Cook over direct heat for 2½ minutes, stirring to prevent sticking. Set aside. Press lingonberry preserves through a sieve. Add sifted preserves to cooked farina. Cool to lukewarm. Beat with electric mixer or rotary beater until thick and fluffy. Pour into serving dishes. Chill. Serve with whipped cream, if desired. Yields 8 one-half-cup servings.

Russia

HOLIDAY HONEY-RYE COOKIES

1 cup honey
½ cup sifted rye flour

½ cup sifted cake flour
½ tsp. salt

Can be frozen. Heat honey to boiling. Mix flours and salt in a skillet, and heat gently, stirring constantly. Remove from heat, and gradually stir in honey. Cool until stiff enough to roll. Then roll paper-thin on floured board, and cut in 2-inch rounds. Bake on greased cooky sheets in 350° F. oven, 10 to 12 minutes. Let stand a minute or two before removing from sheets. Makes about 4 dozen.

Scotland

SHORTBREAD

1 cup butter	½ cup granulated sugar
2 cups flour	Citron or orange peel

Cream the butter thoroughly. Then add the sugar and work together until mixed. Sift the flour and gradually work it into the butter and sugar until the dough is of the consistency of short pastry. The less kneading, the better. Do not roll the dough but press with the hands into two round cakes. Place on a buttered cooky sheet. Pinch the edges neatly with thumb and finger, and prick all over with a fork. Decorate with strips of citron or orange peel. Bake in a hot oven, 400° F., until a light, golden brown.

Sweden

SWEDISH TEA CAKES

½ cup butter	1 egg white
¼ cup brown sugar	½ cup chopped walnuts
1 cup sifted flour	Jelly
1 egg yolk, slightly beaten	

Cream butter and blend in sugar. Add egg yolk, then flour. Roll dough into small balls (1 inch in diameter). Dip in egg white, then roll in chopped nuts. Place on greased cooky sheet and press centers down with spatula. Bake 5 minutes in 300-degree oven. Remove and press down centers again. Bake 15 minutes longer. Cool slightly. Fill centers with jelly.

LUSSEKAKE (Buns honoring Saint Lucia)

2 tbsp. boiling water	½ cup sugar
½ tsp. crumbled saffron threads	1 tsp. salt
1 pkg. active dry yeast	1 cup milk, scalded
¼ cup warm water (110 degrees)	4 cups sifted flour
½ cup butter or margarine	1 egg, well beaten

Pour boiling water on saffron and let stand. Add yeast to ¼ cup of warm water, stirring until dissolved. Let stand 5 to 10 minutes. Meanwhile put butter, sugar, and salt into large bowl, add scalded milk and stir until butter melts. Let stand until lukewarm and then blend in one cup of the flour. Beat smooth. Add yeast and mix well. Add about half the remaining flour and beat smooth. Beat in saffron-water mixture and egg. Add enough remaining flour to make a soft dough. Turn out on floured board. Let " rest " 5 to 10 minutes. Knead until smooth and elastic. Place in greased bowl, cover and let rise in warm place until doubled. Punch down. Make each bun with 2 strips of dough, 4 inches long and ¼ inch in diameter. Form each strip into an S, coiling the ends snail fashion. Place one diagonally across each other, pressing together in center. Place a raisin in center of each coil. Cover and let rise until doubled. Bake at 375 degrees for 15 to 20 minutes. Makes 24 buns.

Switzerland

SWISS CHRISTMAS BREAD

2 tbsp. nuts	½ tsp. salt
¼ cup raisins	¼ tsp. nutmeg
¼ cup candied cherries	⅛ tsp. cloves
2 tbsp. citron	¼ cup hot water
1 package yeast	⅓ cup nonfat milk solids
¼ cup warm water	3 cups sifted all-purpose flour
2 tbsp. butter or margarine	(approximately)
2 tbsp. sugar	1 egg, beaten

Chop nuts and fruit. Soften yeast in warm water. Add butter, sugar, salt, and spices to hot water and cool to lukewarm. Combine nonfat milk solids and 1 cup flour and add to the above mixture; add egg and softened yeast. Mix until smooth. Stir in nuts and fruits. Add the remaining flour gradually until a soft dough is formed. Turn dough out on a lightly floured pastry cloth and knead until smooth. Place dough in a greased bowl and turn once to bring greased side up. Cover and let rise until double in bulk (about 1 hour). Turn dough out on a pastry cloth and divide into 2 parts. Shape into loaves and place in greased loaf pans 7½ x 4 x 2½ inches. Bake in a moderate oven (350° F.) for 40 minutes. Yield: Two small loaves.

LINZER TORTE (*Linzer Tart*)

1 cup almonds	½ tsp. baking powder
1 cup sugar	1 jar raspberry jam
1 cup flour	1 tsp. cinnamon
1 tbsp. chocolate or cocoa	2 small eggs
¼ lb. butter	

Put the sugar, flour, grated almonds, cinnamon, cocoa, and butter in mixing bowl and work thoroughly together as for pie dough. Then add the 2 eggs, cover the bowl, and let rest for 1 hour. Divide the dough into 3 parts. Roll out 2 parts and put into a pie pan. Cover the dough with the raspberry jam. Roll out the third part, cut into very thin strips, and put these crosswise on top of the jam. Bake in a hot oven (400° F.) for 45 minutes.

The United States

Since traditional fruitcake and other Christmas recipes are widely available, we note here only some novel suggestions that have been appreciatively welcomed in many circles for serving fruitcake, a recipe for Yuletide Kisses, one for an uncooked Christmas Plum Pudding, and a Last Minute No-Bake Coconut Fruitcake.

FRUITCAKES
(*Two ways to serve them*)

Either home-baked or those which come from the grocer's shelves take on an air of individuality when served warm with a tangy lemon sauce. Wrap the cake securely in a double thickness of foil and place on a cooky sheet. Heat in slow oven (325° F.) about 40 minutes. Serve with Lemon Fluff Sauce.

LEMON FLUFF SAUCE

1 package lemon-pie filling   2 egg whites, room tempera-
½ cup sugar   ture

Prepare lemon-pie filling mix as directed. Beat egg whites until they form soft peaks. Add sugar a tablespoon at a time and
beat well after each addition. Fold egg whites into lemon mixture and serve warm on heated cake slices. Sauce for 8 servings.

FRUITCAKE SLICES WITH ICE-CREAM CUTOUTS

If you prefer a cold dessert, try this:

1 packaged fruitcake   1 quart vanilla ice cream
Maraschino cherries   Tinted whipped cream

Slice a brick of vanilla ice cream into ½-inch pieces and cut
out shapes with cooky cutters dipped in cold water. Decorate
tops of designs with cherry bits or tinted whipped cream put
through a pastry tube. Place them on foil in the freezer until
ready to serve on fruitcake slices.

YULETIDE KISSES

4 egg whites   ½ tsp. vanilla
Pinch of salt   1 cup coarsely chopped nuts
1 cup sugar

Add the salt to the egg whites and beat the mixture until stiff.
Then add the sugar and vanilla. Continue beating the mixture
only long enough to mix the sugar with the other ingredients.
Stir in the nuts. Cover a baking sheet or pan with a piece of wax
paper (unbuttered). By means of a teaspoon, drop this mixture
on the paper-covered pan in small mounds. Decorate the top
of each cake with one red cinnamon candy surrounded by four
thin slices of angelica, representing green leaves of a flower.
Bake at 300° F. for 25 minutes. Yield: 40 to 50 cakes.

CHRISTMAS PLUM PUDDING
(*Uncooked, with gelatin base*)

1½ tsp. unflavored gelatin	1 cup cold water
½ cup currants	3 egg whites
1 pint milk	½ cup sugar
1½ squares chocolate	¾ cup dates
½ tsp. vanilla	½ cup nuts
1 cup seeded raisins	Salt

Soak gelatin in cold water about 5 minutes. Put milk with fruit in double boiler. When hot, add chocolate which has been melted with part of the sugar, and a little milk added to make a smooth paste. Add soaked gelatin, sugar, salt. Remove from fire, and when mixture begins to thicken, add vanilla and nut meats, chopped, and lastly fold in the whites of eggs, beaten stiff. Turn into a wet mold, lined with whole nut meats and raisins. Chill. Serve with whipped cream, sweetened and flavored with vanilla, or with currant jelly or hard sauce.

LAST MINUTE NO-BAKE COCONUT FRUITCAKE

½ cup golden raisins	Maraschino cherries, halved
¼ cup grape juice	Pecan halves
1 pkg. vanilla pudding and pie filling	¾ cup dry almond macaroon crumbs
2 cups milk	½ cup coarsely chopped pecans
1 tsp. vanilla	½ cup sliced pitted dates
1⅓ cups (about) flaked coconut	¾ cup heavy cream, whipped

Soak raisins overnight. Combine pudding mix and milk in saucepan. Cook and stir over medium heat until mixture comes to a *full* boil. Remove from heat. Add vanilla and coconut. Cool. Oil a 1½-quart loaf or Turk's-head pan lightly. Arrange maraschino cherry halves and pecan halves in a design on bottom of pan. Fold raisins, nuts, dates, and macaroon crumbs into cooled pudding. Then fold in whipped cream. Spoon mixture lightly over design in pan. Freeze eight hours or until firm. Garnish with additional pecan halves and maraschino cherries, if desired. Yield: 10 to 12 portions.

Yugoslavia (Jugoslavia)
HAZELNUT HOLIDAY COOKIES

1 cup butter	2 tsp. vanilla
1 cup hazelnuts, chopped	3 cups flour
1 cup sugar	

Mix ingredients and roll out ½ inch thick and cut in any shape desired. Bake in moderate oven for 20 minutes. Sprinkle with powdered sugar.

10. Christmas Customs
in Christmas Programs

THE CUSTOMS of various countries can be presented effectively in connection with Christmas programs for churches, schools, clubs, or community groups. An example of how this can be done is provided below. This program is based largely on a presentation successfully offered at a Webster Groves, Missouri, church.

THE CHRISTMAS OF MANY PEOPLES

LEADER:

We have before us the Candle of Life, which has been lighted with the Light of Jesus. (*Leader holds up a fairsized candle.*) With this we can send forth light into the darkness, and everyone who accepts this light will find warmth and comfort.

Let us think together about the many peoples all over the world who are observing this Christmas holiday. Because of their differences in culture, they have different ways of worshiping and of observing the birth of Christ.

We shall observe the Italian, the Chinese, the German, the French, the English, and finally the American, Christmas. Each country has something different that it has contributed to this holiday.

AN ITALIAN CHRISTMAS

The group will join in singing " Adestes Fideles."

FIRST SPEAKER (*lights candle 6*):

The song that we have just sung is only a sample of the rich Latin background of Italy. Italy is rich with beautiful music telling of the birth of Christ. Among many others, we owe to these people the immortal anthem " Gesu Bambino."

Three weeks constitute the Christmas season in Italy, which starts eight days before our Christmas Day. During this period, children go from place to place reciting Christmas selections, expecting coins with which to purchase special delicacies of the season. Many go around playing musical instruments and singing carols.

While a rigid fast is observed the twenty-four hours preceding Christmas Eve, it is followed by as elaborate a banquet as can be afforded. Then follows the drawing of presents from the " Urn of Fate." Though many blanks are included, and these merely add to the merriment, ultimately a present for each one is provided. At sunset the booming of cannons from the Castle of St. Angelo proclaims the opening of the holy season. By eight o'clock all the people attend church to behold the procession of church officials in their beautiful robes and to participate in the celebration of the Christmas Eve mass.

A CHINESE CHRISTMAS

The group sings the carol — " Sweet and Holy Jesus' Name." This is found in *Carols, Customs and Costumes Around the World.*

SECOND SPEAKER (*lights candle 1*):

Sheng Dan Jieh, or the Holy Birth Festival, as the Chinese call Christmas, is penetrating more than one thousand miles into the interior of China. Evergreens, holly, and a great variety of paper decorations adorn churches and homes. Paper chains in green, red, yellow, and blue are suspended in interlocking festoons overhead. On the white walls are posted large elaborate characters meaning " Peace " and " Joy." In front stands the Tree of Life, as the Chinese call the Christmas Tree. It has no candles, but it is decked with paper flowers, colored paper chains, paper bells, and cotton snowflakes.

In some cities a parade of some 150 people proclaim the Christmas message through banners and songs by marching for several miles through the main streets at midday. Some have established the custom of a common Christmas meal.

The Chinese make much of distributing gifts of food, clothing, and money to the homes of needy villagers, or sending gifts to neighboring provinces where there is suffering from famine, plague, or some other affliction. Their Santa Claus is mostly one who takes care of the needy, and he is very real and alive to them. (While the above picture no doubt has been modified in recent years, much of it continues, especially in Hong Kong.)

A GERMAN CHRISTMAS

The group joins in " Silent Night! Holy Night! "

THIRD SPEAKER (*lights candle 5*):

One of our most loved of all carols, " Silent Night! Holy Night! " comes to us from Germany. There the Christmas observance starts with Saint Nicholas' Day which is December 6. They usually have a large tree for each family. Usually the mother does the trimming and provides the table for the gifts; she will not admit anyone else into the special room until 8 o'clock on Christmas Eve, when everyone comes to view the tree decorated with shiny tinsel, bright-colored balls, and cookies baked into the shape of men, women, animals, and the like. The family then spends the evening around the beauty of the tree, singing carols and opening their gifts.

On Christmas Eve and again on Christmas morning the families attend Christmas services at their churches.

A French Christmas

The group sings " Angels, We Have Heard on High."
FOURTH SPEAKER (*lights candle 2*):

The French observe Christmas Eve by staying up all night to welcome Christmas, very much as we do on New Year's Eve. They invite friends and celebrate the birthday of Christ joyously. The children place their shoes on the hearth for Petit Noël, the Christ-child, to fill them with gifts.

Several days previous to Christmas, the children go into the fields and woods to gather laurel, holly, bright berries, and pretty greenery with which to build the crèche, a representation of the manger. After the ceremony of lighting the yule log on Christmas Eve, the children light up the crèche with small candles.

An English Christmas

The group sings " The First Nowell."
FIFTH SPEAKER (*lights candle 4*):

Of all countries, England has probably celebrated the merriest of yuletides. It is the land of the yule log, the plum pudding, the boar's head, the Christmas carol, and the Christmas card. The stockings are hung at the chimney with care for Father Christmas to fill.

On the afternoon of the day before Christmas comes the solemn occasion of uprooting the fir tree from the garden, planting it in the big Christmas tub, and bringing it into the corner of the living room. Since the same tree is used for years, it becomes an old friend.

Christmas Day begins with the children's early search for their stockings. The morning is then given over to religious services which are followed by family dinners. Only after afternoon tea is the living room opened and all rush in to admire the tree ablaze with its colored lights and to share in the gifts piled high on the table directly beside the tree. When the last gift has been opened, the remaining hours are spent in playing games and telling stories. The reading of Dickens' A Christmas Carol is generally an event of the day.

General gift-giving does not occur until the day after Christmas, known as Boxing Day, for the reason that it is on this day that servants and the poor receive money gifts in little boxes.

AN AMERICAN CHRISTMAS

The group sings " O Little Town of Bethlehem."
SIXTH SPEAKER (lights candle 3):
     The American Christmas that most of us know is composed of threads from many countries woven into a beautiful tapestry, reflecting in modified form the customs of many and widely separated lands in church and home and shop.

As has been said, our Christmas cards, our yule logs, our boars' heads, our plum puddings from England; our Santa Claus from Holland; our stockings hung at the fireplace, the Christmas tree, and many other traditions observed during our Christmas season reflect foreign cultures. The turkey seems to be our only contribution, materially speaking, to Christmas.

Greater than all these customs and rituals that we observe is the real nature of the holiday. It is so easy to celebrate it with hardly an inkling as to its real meaning. We unconsciously think of Christmas only as a day for Santa Claus, gifts, and a merry time. But it becomes a really significant day only when we remember that it is the birthday of Jesus, God's gift to mankind. This " unspeakable gift " continues to inspire men and nations also in our day.

CONCLUSION. (*Use " A Merry Christmas " in several languages. See pages 37–38.*)

Bibliography

CHRISTMAS CUSTOMS

Gardner, Horace J. *Let's Celebrate Christmas.* 212 pp. The Ronald Press Company, 1940.

Krythe, M. R. *All About Christmas.* 211 pp. Harper & Brothers, 1954.

Sechrist, E. H. *Christmas Everywhere.* 176 pp. Macrae-Smith Company, 1936.

Then, John N. *Christmas.* 154 pp. Bruce Publishing Company, 1934.

Wernecke, H. H. *Carols, Customs and Costumes Around the World.* 48 pp. Old Orchard Publishers, 1936.

CHRISTMAS DECORATIONS AND PARTIES

Baer, Barbara. *Christmas Make-It Book.* 96 pp. H. Wolff, 1954.

Biddle, Dorothy. *Christmas Idea Book.* 221 pp. M. Barrows, 1953.

Today's Woman, Ideas for Christmas. 144 pp. Fawcett Publications, 1953.

Wertsner, Anne. *Make Your Own Merry Christmas.* 127 pp. Fawcett Publications, 1946.

CHRISTMAS SONGS

Simon, Henry (ed.) *A Treasury of Songs and Carols.* 243 pp. Houghton Mifflin Company, 1955.

Taylor, C. (ed.) *The Hawthorn Book of Christmas Carols.* Hawthorn Books, 1957.

Wasner, F. *Trapp-Family Book of Christmas Songs.* 129 pp. Pantheon Books, 1950.

Wernecke, H. H. *Christmas Songs and Their Stories.* 128 pp. The Westminster Press, 1957.
—— *Carols, Customs and Costumes Around the World.* 48 pp. Old Orchard Publishers, 1936.
—— *Favorite Christmas, Folk and Sacred Songs.* 32 pp. Old Orchard Press, n.d.
Wheeler, O. *Sing for Christmas.* 125 pp. E. P. Dutton, 1943.

CHRISTMAS STORIES

Bishop, A. H. *Happy Christmas, Tales for Boys and Girls.* 285 pp. Stephen Daye Press, 1956.
Eggleston, M. W. *The Red Stocking and Other Christmas Stories.* 153 pp. Harper & Brothers, 1937.
Menotti. *Amahl and the Night Visitors.* 86 pp. McGraw-Hill Book Co., Inc., 1927.
Posselt, Eric. *The World's Greatest Christmas Stories.* 451 pp. Ziff-Davis, 1949.
Sangster, Margaret. *The Littlest Orphan and Other Christmas Stories.* 150 pp. Round Table Press, 1935.
Van Buren, Maud. *Christmas in Storyland.* 328 pp. Century Co., 1927.
Wagenknecht, Edward. *The Fireside Book of Christmas Stories.* 659 pp. The Bobbs-Merrill Company, Publishers, 1945.

Indexes

Index by Countries

Abyssinia, 101 f.
  Coptic liturgy, 101 f.

Alaska, 74

Algiers, 102
  French cafés, 102
  midnight mass, 102

Arabia, 112 f.
  foreigners' Christmas ob-
    servance, 112 f.

Argentina, 89 f.
  Christmas Eve or morning
    mass, 89 f.

Armenia (Old), 113 f.
  fasting, then feasting, 113 f.
  Recipe: Pilav, 154

Australia, 133 ff.
  Christmas bell, 134
  Christmas bush, 134

Austria, 43 f.
  Christmas Eve dinner, 44
  midnight mass, 44
  " Showing the Christ-
    child," 44
  " Turmblasen," 44

Belgium, 44 ff.
  Christmas plays, 45 f.
  Christmas processions, 44 ff.

Bohemia. See Czechoslovakia

Brazil, 90 ff.
  the mass and the manger, 90
  Papa Noël, 91
  white-gift Christmas, 92

Bulgaria, 46
  Christmas wish ceremony,
    46

Canada, 77 ff.
  Labrador, 78
  Newfoundland, 78
  Nova Scotia, 78
  Vancouver, 78 f.

Central America, 80 ff.

Ceylon, 135 f.
  Christian Christmas, 135 f.
  pagan superstitions, 135 f.

Chile
  Virgin del Rosario, 94

China (Old), 136 ff.
  Christmas and the Chinese
    New Year, 137 ff.

Columbia, 94 ff.
  aguinaldos (gifts), 95
  carols, 95
  Recipe: Bunuelos (dessert),
    154

Congo, 102 ff.
  Nativity story, 103 f.

Costa Rica, 81

Czechoslovakia, 46 f.
  manger, 47
  midnight mass, 47
  Svatej Nikulas Day, Dec. 6,
    46
  Three Kings' Day, Jan. 6,
    46

Recipe: Kolage (coffee-
    cake), 155

Denmark
  Christmas seals, 34
  Recipe: Danish Julekake,
    155

Dominican Republic, 81

England. See Great Britain

Ethiopia. See Abyssinia

Formosa, 140 ff.
  family meals, 142
  greeting cards, 142

France, 47 f.
  Father Christmas, 47, 91
  manger, 47
  midnight mass, 47
  Saint Nicholas Day, Dec. 6,
    47
  santons (little saints), 47
  Recipe: Petits gateaux tailles
    (cookies), 157

Germany, 48 f.
  Advent candles, wreaths,
    31, 48
  Christkind, 49
  Christmas tree, 48
  Knecht Ruprecht, 49
  Recipes:
    German Christmas cook-
      ies, 157
    Lebkuchen, 158

Pfeffernuesse (ginger-
bread), 158
Springerle (cookies), 159

Ghana, 104 ff.
Christian Christmas, 105 ff.

Great Britain, 49 ff.
boar's head, 32
cards, 33
carols, 32
Christmas dinner, 50
Christmas stocking, 35 f.
mistletoe, 19
wassail bowl, 37
yule log, 29 ff.
Recipes:
English Christmas bread,
156
Yorkshire salad, 156 f.

Greece, 51
carols with drums, 51
Christpsomo, bread of
Christ, 51
Recipe: Tea biscuit, 159

Hawaii, 74 f.
outdoor observance of
Christmas, 74
Recipe: Chicken curry,
159 f.

Holland, 52 f.
Christmas music, 53
Christmas shoes, 36
St. Nicholas, 52 f.

St. Nicholas Day, Dec. 6,
52
St. Nicholas parade, 52 f.

Honduras, 82

Hungary, 53 f.
Saint Nicholas, 53
two-day church holiday,
53 f.
Recipe: Christmas seed
cookies, 160

India, 114 ff.
Christmas adaptations,
114 ff.

Indians, American, 75 ff.
Navahos, New Mexico, 76
Pimas, Arizona, 76 f.

Iran, 120
Christmas (the Little
Feast), 120

Ireland, 50
candles in windows, 50
" Feeding the Wren," 50
Recipe: Soda scones, 160

Israel, 121 ff.
Christmas Eve, 122 ff.
Church of the Nativity,
122 ff.
Shepherds' Fields, 122,
124 f.

Italy, 54 f.
Befana, Epiphany, Jan. 6,
55

Italy (*cont.*)
  presepios, 54
  Recipe: Christmas bread,
    161

Japan, 142 ff.
  Christian mission Christ-
    mas, 143 ff.
  Christmas, a secular festi-
    val, 142 f.

Korea, 145 ff.
  Christmas common in,
    145 f.

Labrador, 78

Lebanon, 125 ff.

Liberia, 107 f.
  mission Christmas observ-
    ance, 107 f.

Lithuania, 55
  straw-covered dinner table,
    55
  wafer symbolizing love, 55

Mexico, 82 ff.
  piñata, 84 f.
  posadas, 82 ff.
  Recipe: Orange thins,
    161 f.

Newfoundland, 78
  fishing for the church, 78

New Guinea, 147 ff.
  Christmas worship in a hos-
    pital, 157 ff.

New Zealand, 149 ff.
  midsummer Christmas,
    149 ff.
  See also Australia, Central
    America, Ghana, Ha-
    waii, and others

Nicaragua, 85 f.

Norway, 57, 60
  Recipes:
    Lingonberry mousse, 162
    Sand kager, 162

Nova Scotia, 78

Pakistan, 129 f.
  family festival, 129 f.

Palestine. *See* Israel

Panama, 86 f.
  aguinaldos (gifts), 87
  Nacimientos, 87

Persia. *See* Iran

Peru, 96 f.
  Lima, "City of One Hun-
    dred Churches," 96 f.

Philippines, 75
  fireworks, 75
  lantern contest, 75
  pastores (plays), 75

Poland. *See* Czechoslovakia

Puerto Rico, 87 f.

Rumania, 55 f.
  coaxing trees to bear, 55
  plays, 56
  priestly blessings at Epiphany, 56

Russia (Old), 56 f.
  Grandfather Frost, 57
  homes blessed by priests, 57
  Recipe: Holiday honey-rye cookies, 162

Scandinavia, 57 ff.
  Julebukk, 60
  lutfisk, 58
  St. Knut's Day, Jan. 13, 57, 60 f.
  St. Lucia's Day, Dec. 13, 57 f.
  sheaf of grain, 37, 58

Scotland, 50
  New Year's family reunions, 50
  Recipe: Shortbread, 163

Serbia, 61 f.
  family kiss, 62
  roasted pig, 61
  yule log, 61

Siberia, 62
  exiles fed, 62

Spain, 62 f.
  Nacimiento, 63
  Noche Buena (good night), 62

Sweden, 57 ff.
  Recipes:
    Lussekake, 163
    Tea cakes, 163

Switzerland, 64 ff.
  Christkindli, 64 f.
  church bells, 64
  church services, 64
  Tirggel (cookies), 65
  Recipes:
    Linzer torte, 165
    Swiss Christmas bread, 164 f.

Syria, 130 ff.
  Bethlehem pilgrimage, 131
  St. Barbara's Day, Dec. 4, 130 f.

Turkey, 66
  home of St. Nicholas, the bishop, 66

Ukrainia, 66 f.
  caroling, 67
  Christmas on Jan. 6 (Julian calendar), 66
  midnight mass, 67
  "The star!" 67

Union of South Africa, 108 ff.
  immigrant peoples, 108 ff.
  unchristianized natives, 108 ff.
  the younger churches, 108 ff.

United States of America,
    69 ff.
Alaska, 74
Christmas seals, 34 f.
Christmas, town names,
    39 f.
Christmas trees, commu-
    nity. See Subject index
Dutch Christmas, Manhat-
    tan, 72
Hawaii, 74 f.
Jamestown (1607), 70 f.
Moravian Christmas, 72 f.
New Amsterdam, 72 f.
Old South, 73 f.
Philippines, 75
Pilgrims, 71 f.
Plymouth (1620), 71
Santa Claus, Ind., 41
Yule log, 29 ff.
Recipes:
    Lemon fluff sauce, 166

    No-bake coconut fruit-
        cake, 167 f.
    Plum pudding (gelatin
        base), 167
    Yuletide kisses, 166

Vancouver, 78 f.

Venezuela, 97 f.
    mass: morning, midnight,
        97
    Nacimiento (crib), 97

Wales, 50 f.
    carol-singing, 50 f.
    Christmas goose, 51
    taffy-making, 51

Yugoslavia, 67 f.
    Kolache (coffeecake), 68
    yule log, 67 f.
    Recipe: Hazelnut holiday
        cookies, 168

Index by Subjects and Names

Advent:
  candles, 31
  wreaths, 31

African leper hospital, 100 f.

Alaska, "Going round with the star," 74

Bells, 28 f.

Bells, Switzerland, 64

Bethlehem, Christmas at, 121 ff.

Bethlehem, pilgrimage to, 131

Boar's head, 32

Brooks, Phillips, 11

Candles, 24 f., 31

Candles, Czechoslovakia, 46

Carols and caroling, 32 f.

Christkind, 49

Christmas cards, 33 f.

Christmas presents, 36

Christmas rose, 20

Christmas seals, 34 f.

Christmas songs:
  "The earth has grown old," 11
  "We Three Kings of Orient Are," 26

Christmas stocking, 35 f.

"Christmas," town names:
    Arizona, Florida, Kentucky,
    Mississippi, Nova Scotia,
    Tennessee, 39

Christmas tree, Germany, 48

Christmas tree, community:
    Altadena, Calif., 22
    Bellingham, Wash., 23
    Bethlehem, Pa., 26
    Denver, Colo., 25
    Kansas City, Mo., 25
    Los Angeles, Calif., 23
    New York, N.Y., 22
    Northport, Wash., 23
    Palmer Lake, Colo., 26
    Pasadena, Calif., 22
    Philadelphia, Pa., 22
    Rockefeller Center, N.Y.,
        23
    Van Nuys, Calif., 26
    Washington, D.C., 22

"Christmas" village, 40

Colored flames for fireplaces,
    29 f.

Cookies. See Recipes

Coptic liturgy, 101 f.

December 25, 13

Epiphany, 55

Eskimo Christmas, 77

Father Christmas, 47

Feast of Lights, 24 f.

Grenfell, Wilfred T., 78

Guest, Edgar A., 12

Holly, 18 f.

Indians, 75 ff.
    Navahos, New Mexico, 76
    Pimas, Arizona, 76 f.

Jamestown (1607), 70 f.

Joseph and the cherry tree,
    19 f.

Knecht Ruprecht, 49

Lake Placid, 41

Leper hospital Christmas,
    100 ff.

Lutfisk, 58

Manger:
    Brazil, 90 f.
    Czechoslovakia, *jeslicky*, 27,
        47
    France, *crèche*, 27
    Germany, *Krippe*, 27
    Italy, *presepio*, 27
    Spain, *Nacimiento*, 27, 63

Manhattan, 72

"Merry Christmas" as others say it, 37 ff.

Mission Christmas observances:
Africa, leper hospital, 100 ff.
Brazil, 92
Ceylon, 135 f.
China (Old), 138 ff.
Congo, 103 ff.
Formosa, 141 f.
Ghana, 104 ff.
India, 115 ff.
Japan, 143 ff.
Korea, 146 f.
Liberia, 107 f.
New Guinea, 147 ff.

Mistletoe, 19

Moravians, 72 f.

Nacimiento (crib), 27, 63, 87, 97

Navahos, 76

New Amsterdam, 72

Old South, 73 f.

Origen, 13

Papa Noël, 91

Pennsylvania Germans, 73

Piñata, Mexico, 84

Plymouth (1620), 71

Poems:
"The Christmas Tree," 23

"The earth has grown old," 11

"A man is at his finest," 12

Poinsettia, 40

Posadas, Mexico, 82 f., 84 f.

Presepios, 54, 91

Puritans, 28, 71 f.

Recipes:
Bunuelos, dessert from Columbia, 154
Christmas seed cookies, Hungary, 160
Curry, chicken, Hawaii, 159 f.
Danish Julekake, 155
English Christmas bread, 156
Fruitcake, no-bake, 167 f.
Fruitcake serving, 165
German Christmas cookies, 157 f.
Hazelnut holiday cookies, Yugoslavia, 168
Italian Christmas bread, 161
Kolage, coffeecake, Czechoslovakia, 155
Lebkuchen, Germany, 158
Lemon fluff sauce, U.S., 166
Lingonberry mousse, Norway, 162
Linzer torte, Switzerland, 165

Recipes (*cont.*)
Lussekake, Sweden, 163
Orange thins, Mexico, 161 f.
Petits gateaux tailles, French cookies, 157
Pfeffernuesse (gingerbread), Germany, 158
Pilav, Armenia, 154
Plum pudding, gelatin, U.S., 167
Rye cookies, Russia, 162
Sand kager, Norway, 162
Soda scones, Ireland, 160
Shortbread, Scotland, 163
Springerle, Germany, 159
Swedish tea cakes, 163
Swiss Christmas bread, 164 f.
Tea biscuit, Greece, 159
Yorkshire salad, England, 156 f.
Yuletide kisses, U.S., 166

Saint Barbara's Day, Dec. 4, 130 f.

Saint Knut's Day, Jan. 13, 57, 60 f.

Saint Lucia's Day, 57 f.

Saint Nicholas, Turkey, 66

Saint Nicholas, *Papa Noël*, Brazil, 91

Saint Nicholas, name variations, 40

Saint Nicholas Day, Dec. 6, France, 47

Santa Claus, Ind., 41

Santa Claus, origin, 16 ff.

Santa's Workshop, Wilmington, N.Y., 41 f.

Secularizing Christmas, 13 ff.

Santons (little saints), 47

Sheaf of grain, 37

Songs. *See* Christmas

South, Old, 73 f.

Star of Bethlehem, 25 f.

Telesphorus, Bishop of Rome, 13

Three Kings' Day:
Argentina, 90
Czechoslovakia, 46
Puerto Rico, 88

Tinsel, 20

Torrington, Conn., 40

"Turmblasen," Austria, 44

Wassail bowl, 37

"We Three Kings of Orient Are," 26

White-gift Christmas, Brazil, 92

Wreaths, 31, 48

Yule log, 29 ff., 61, 67 f.